A CHRISTIAN APPROACH TO
ECONOMICS AND THE CULTURAL CONDITION

Books by Douglas Vickers

A CHRISTIAN APPROACH TO ECONOMICS AND THE
CULTURAL CONDITION
NOW THAT YOU HAVE BELIEVED: AN EXPLORATION OF THE
LIFE AND WALK OF FAITH
MAN IN THE MAELSTROM OF MODERN THOUGHT
ECONOMICS AND MAN: PRELUDE TO A CHRISTIAN CRITIQUE
STUDIES IN THE THEORY OF MONEY, 1690-1776
THE THEORY OF THE FIRM: PRODUCTION, CAPITAL, AND FINANCE
FINANCIAL MARKETS IN THE CAPITALIST PROCESS
CORNELIUS VAN TIL AND THE THEOLOGIAN'S THEOLOGICAL STANCE

Contributing Author

ESSAYS ON ADAM SMITH
A STUDY OF MUTUAL FUNDS
MODERN ECONOMIC THOUGHT

A CHRISTIAN APPROACH TO ECONOMICS AND THE CULTURAL CONDITION

Douglas Vickers

AN EXPOSITION-UNIVERSITY BOOK

Exposition Press   Smithtown, New York

FIRST EDITION

© 1982 by Douglas Vickers

All rights reserved. No part of this book may be reproduced, in whole or in part, in any form or by any means, electronic or mechanical, including photocopying, recording, or by any information storage and retrieval system, without permission in writing from the publisher. Address inquiries to Exposition Press, Inc., 325 Rabro Drive, Smithtown, NY 11787-0817.

Library of Congress Catalog Card Number: 81-86526

ISBN 0-682-49831-9

Printed in the United States of America

To
JOHN SKILTON
with gratitude for
his many kindnesses

Contents

Preface ix

1 Introduction and Reader's Guide 1
2 The Problem 14
3 The Intellectual–Cultural Condition 33
4 The Economists' Perspective 51
5 The Roots of Economic Culture 79
6 Economics, Culture, and Rationality 117
7 The Problem Revisited 149

Notes 183

Index 195

Preface

In this book I have attempted to establish a perspective, a critical vantage point, from which to view the relations between economic thought and the evaluative thought forms of Christian belief. Trends and developments on the first of these levels have made significant contributions to cultural and societal formations, and it is necessary, for a clear understanding of the meaning of the times, to bring to bear on them the searchlight of biblical Christianity. A summary of the details of the argument, the scope of the work, and the methods of analysis I have adopted are given in the first chapter, and I have included there also a reader's guide to the book. That chapter will eliminate the need for any further prefatory observations.

I have incurred a heavy debt to those friends and colleagues who have read and commented on the work, in particular to Professors John Mason and Bruce Webb. In expressing my gratitude I absolve them from responsibility for whatever infelicities remain. Parts of the analysis in the book have been based on more extensive discussions of some of the same themes in two of my previous books, *Man in the Maelstrom of Modern Thought* (Presbyterian and Reformed Publishing Company) and *Economics and Man: Prelude to a Christian Critique* (Craig Press). I am grateful to Mr. Charles Craig of those publishing companies for permission to draw on that previous work and reproduce here some of that published material.

1

Introduction and Reader's Guide

This work is concerned essentially with a single objective, that of examining the forms and structures of economic culture and economic problems, policies, and theories on the one hand, and the relevance and prescriptive competence of some important thought forms of Christian belief on the other. But larger issues are necessarily involved, and our argument will broaden to a wider consideration of some important culture-forming aspects of intellectual history and their significance for the present state of affairs.

The task is not a new one, and a number of the important essays that have been addressed to it in earlier times will be referred to throughout the argument. But the analysis that follows will, it is hoped, be differentiated in respects that at this time are critically necessary for the sound evaluation of our condition. First, it is important to acknowledge that the development of our intellectual systems has brought us to a point at which a remarkable confluence has occurred between the philosophic and sociocultural concerns for man, his status, conditions, and prospects, and the essential and enduring concerns of Christian theology and belief. The question before us is the question of man, his cultural structures—in our case particularly his economic structures—his security, place, and hopes, and the interpretative data that, as the problem of man is addressed, are provided by

Christian belief. In the early chapters of this work attention will therefore be given to certain larger determinants of our cultural history and condition that illuminate this relation.

Second, those critical categories and the diagnostic relations that Christian thought provides must be seen to be grounded in the biblical data, and accordingly in the revelatory thought forms that God in His providence has provided. These issues coalesce in the explanation of what will be referred to as the pervasive existentialist and nihilist milieu of our thought and culture, and of what will be termed the rationalist-irrationalist dialecticism of the age. The terms will be discussed and explained in the two chapters that follow. For the present it is noted that in the ongoing discussion the biblical data will be invoked in an explicit and determinative way.

Third, it is necessary to note that although the analysis is concerned with the contiguity and interdependence between economic and Christian thought, it is beyond the scope of our objectives to construct either a systematic theology or an extended or systematic economic theory. That has been done in other places that will be referred to. At this stage a clarification is required of the foundations on which such extensive and systematic works as those can be properly developed. Our concern will be with culturally relevant and biblically informed directions of analysis and with the principal and necessary reasons for coherence among them.

Fourth, it will be necessary for purposes of the analysis to trace out some of the principal highlights of the history of economics as an intellectual discipline and to discover the primary motivations and concerns that have brought it to its present developed state. In the course of doing so, notice will be taken of the instances and manner in which the outstanding architects of the discipline have been influenced by the Christian faith—or, on the contrary, have proceeded in explicit objection to it—and the extent to which they have first explicitly embraced, and then equally explicitly repudiated, that faith. It will be seen that during the formative stages of the development of the discipline in the nineteenth century a number of important predecessors and

Introduction and Reader's Guide

formers of our current intellectual positions fell into the last mentioned category of recanters from theological beliefs.

Fifth, the pressing concerns of socioeconomic inquiry, having to do with property, power, economic stability and growth, freedom and security, equity and opportunity, employment, inflation, class relations, justice, discrimination, and accountability will appear in appropriate perspective in the analysis. So also will the interesting and important dichotomies between socialism and capitalism, and individualism and collectivism. But to start the analysis with an appeal to those latter dichotomies would shunt the inquiry onto a fruitless track before the argument could get under way. For initial attention needs to be paid to deeper springs and motivations of human action than are readily provided by such direct and explicit dichotomies. Man stands, it will be argued, under a covenantal relationship of responsibility to his Creator, and under the economic-cultural mandate that was initially imposed upon him. The construction and the scope of that covenant and mandate are observable in the first chapter of the book of Genesis and will be explored at some length. But although the construction of an extensive and technical economics will be avoided throughout the argument, sufficient formal relations will be provided to illumine the meaning of economics as a discipline to which Christian thought is relevant, and sufficient reference will be made to practical, pressing, and empirical problems to evidence the relevance of the arguments that will be adduced.

Finally, the analysis will conclude with an indication of lines of development and further investigation which, under the formative guidance of God's common grace, call for the collaboration and pursuit of Christian men. A proper recognition of the scope for policy and action in the economic and social arenas will force an awareness of a fundamental distinction in this regard. It will be necessary and important to distinguish carefully, in all aspects of economic and social action and policy, between the prerogatives and responsibilities of the church as the church on the one hand, and the prerogatives and responsibilities of Christian men as Christian men on the other. Confusion of the right limits of action on these different levels of responsibility has occasioned all too much error in the past.

The question of whether a particular form of economic arrangements for society, for example socialism or capitalism, can be regarded as mandatory or preferred will be explored. The questions of property, power, responsibilities, and the rights consonant with each will be addressed. But a question of deeper concern will be the accordance with biblical data of the elements and building blocks, of both assumption and practice, that are formative of such socioeconomic systems as have just been mentioned. There have existed, in traditional analyses on those levels, a number of deeply ingrained assumptions regarding economic forces and their operation that need carefully to be called in question. The argument can be made, for example, that there is no reason to embrace with confidence what emerged as the classical postulate that if left to itself the economic system would automatically equilibrate at a high and favorable level of employment and generalized economic welfare. On the contrary, it will be argued at some length that any such assumptions of automatic harmonies in the economic system do not accord with the explanatory data of the Scriptures to which appeal is to be made. That is so because economic systems and arrangements are shot through with forces of disequilibrium, change, kaleidic variation, and worrying disturbances, rather than characterized by equilibrium, harmony, and generalized benefit. Careful consideration will accordingly be given to the locus of economic responsibility for stabilizing policies, for the protection of welfare and a scheme of things in which individual energies can be profitably and efficiently put to work. There will be, therefore, a necessary consideration of the economic power and responsibility of the state, based on a prior examination of the genesis and authority of the state as a viable and God-ordained institution.

It will be acknowledged that sin is abroad in the world and in the hearts of men and that it points to economic dislocation and disequilibrium. Against this fact it will be necessary to confront the question whether anything is to be served by introducing what might be called corrective economic policies

Introduction and Reader's Guide

administered by the state. This is a question that properly engages the concern of Christian men who are able to bring to bear on it valuable insights from a wide range of biblical data and presupposition and from empirical and historical awareness. For that reason, the analysis will attempt to set out clearly the properly biblical locus and origin of economic responsibility and stewardship. In that perspective, it will endeavor to answer the question of the responsibility of the state in such a way as to preserve all relevant individual freedoms and obligations, at the same time as the empirical realities of a fallen and sinful world—and the practical policy implications of those realities—are observed. At this introductory point, it can be left for the detailed analysis to show what mixtures and distributions of individual and societally collective responsibilities are necessary and advisable.

The Christian dogma and the biblical data on which it is grounded countenance neither unfettered and rampant individualistic capitalism on the one hand, nor collectivist centralizations on the other. Tensions exist and remain to be carefully explored between freedom and security, equity and responsibility, and between property, power, ownership, and the larger rights of economic benefits and wealth. Foremost among the determinative thought forms that will impel the analysis will be that deriving from the fact that we do not in this age live in an economic theocracy, as was the case in an earlier period, when God brought His people out of the bondage of Egypt to the lands and the destiny He had prepared for them. At that time, those people were given full, explicit, and adequate legislative guidance for the organization and administration of the economic affairs consonant with the theocracy that was thereby established. But we no longer live in that sense in a theocracy. At the initial point of our inquiry we must acknowledge that we live in a fallen world. Sin is abroad in the world and in the hearts of men. And that fact is determinative of the forms and structures and practical potential of the economic arrangements we see around us.

It is against this background that the question of the economic prerogatives and responsibilities of the state will be considered, as a God-ordained institution established within the scope of the operation of His common grace in this fallen world. But our argument will not be statist, in the sense that claims will be made that the state is to be established as the necessary and efficient performer or guide in all of economic production and affairs. It will be acknowledged that the sin that disorders the productive and economic arrangements between men and the economic institutions they construct will, in various ways and for various reasons, be likely also to disturb the nicely balanced behavior and functioning of established state authorities. Sin, unfortunately, will continue to be sin and will continue to be seen to be sin, whether it comes to expression and to economically disturbing effects in either private and individualized, or in governmentally organized, economic arrangements. A proper sorting out of the legitimate natures of both individual responsibility and action and government responsibility will exhibit the wisdom of the Psalmist's dictum: "It is better to trust in the Lord than to put confidence in man." But equally, "It is better to trust in the Lord than to put confidence in princes" (Psalm 118:8-9). This book is an attempt to seek consistently for the proper scriptural balance and sanction in these critically important directions of economic organization and arrangements.

* * *

Against the foregoing sketch of the objectives of this book it will be useful to refer briefly to the contents of the chapters that follow. In the second chapter a somewhat condensed review is given of the principal features of the sociocultural position in which we stand at this time and of the main influences of intellectual and scientific history which have brought us to that position. The categories in terms of which the discussion proceeds are in a fairly rigorous sense philosophic, and the treatment of the material is largely assertive rather than analytical in a detailed sense. Such a procedure has been deliberately adopted as a means of sketching a minimal and essential background and the main features of the framework within which the subsequent more detailed analysis proceeds. For this reason, the argument at this

Introduction and Reader's Guide

initial stage is not extensively related to earlier scholarship, in the sense that such a procedure is adopted as the work gradually unfolds. Moreover, this method of introducing the principal lines of analysis permits the work to exhibit the main features of both the philosophico-theological thought on the one hand, and the economic arguments and concerns on the other. The argument is made, for example, that in a remarkable sense that was not earlier understood to be the case, both theology and economics are incomplete at this time. They are incomplete in the sense that new questions are being raised in place of previously comfortable assurances, old moorings have been vacated, and new lines of investigation have come into vogue.

The introductory argument in the following two chapters incorporates a condensed view of the outlines of what has become known as the epistemological problem, meaning the problem of answering the question, "How do we know?" It is the problem that has to do with the origin, processes, and validity of knowledge. Such an introduction is necessary because of the manner in which, as will become clear, the economics discipline has absorbed the epistemological assumptions of the natural sciences, has adopted decidedly positivistic stances in many of its empirical analyses, and has failed to address itself to the fundamental question of what, if anything, can be properly understood as a biblically informed theory of knowledge and knowledge processes. It will be seen that a highly significant dialecticism exists in contemporary thought in general. It is a dialecticism between epistemological assumptions that comprehensiveness of knowledge is (at least theoretically) attainable on the one hand, and, on the other hand, that the randomness of chance and the stochastic laws that underlie all reality make it possible, in the final logical outcome, to be sure of nothing at all. That important tension in modern thought, that significant dialecticism or swinging back and forth between apparently opposite principles of knowledge, will be examined at some length.

In the third chapter more detailed consideration is given to what is there termed the intellectual-cultural condition. At that stage some definitional statements are made about the pervasively existentialist and nihilist traditions that have come into vogue. The relevant terms are defined there, and the complex of influences that emerge and converge from economic, philosophic, and theological thought are brought into congruence. The material in these second and third chapters, and the rather severely abbreviated manner in which it has been treated, make them probably the most difficult chapters in the book. But the argument contained in them has been presented in the form it has for two reasons. First, in those chapters a large number of categories, terms, concepts, and lines of analysis are raised which are subsequently brought to bear on the illumination of the more narrowly economic analysis that is under review. They therefore provide something of a conceptual vocabulary and an idea-set in terms of which dimensions of the later work can be more fully viewed. Second, in those chapters a fruitful linkage between economic and Christian theological thought (which is the main concern of the remainder of the work) on the one hand, and other aspects of our cultural and social position on the other, is established. In effect, lines of analysis are thereby suggested as to the manner and the directions in which mutually consistent analyses of aspects of the larger cultural and existential condition might profitably be worked out.

Many readers, however, might profitably begin their initial reading of the work with Chapter 4. The work from that point on has been presented in such a way that continuity, coherence, and assimilation can be maintained by noting the manner in which, when thought forms from the earlier chapters are introduced, they are redefined or described sufficiently to preserve continuity and clarity of argument. The main body of the work, that dealing with the relation between economics and Christian thought and belief, is contained in the final four chapters, and if the second and third chapters are skimmed lightly preparatory to a closer reading of Chapters 4 through 7, the latter should be read in the order in which they are presented for purposes of maintaining the optimal sequence of argument and analysis.

Chapter 4, "The Economists' Perspective," discusses the emergence of economics as a separate intellectual discipline in the hands of Adam Smith and his eighteenth-century predecessors. Particular attention is given there to the organizing assumption in the so-called classical economics of the automatic harmonies in the system and the "invisible hand" that was assumed to guarantee their working. The emergence of the notion of laissez-faire and the orthodoxy that quickly surrounded it are observed. Questions are raised as to its descriptive or prescriptive competence in actual economic fact. In this chapter also, deeper attention is given to the manner in which the architects of the economics discipline understood themselves to be forging an autonomous, atheological, amoral science, and the manner in which they did, or did not, envisage their work as being in some sense contiguous with Christian thought. It is at this point of the work that the various historical strands of social and economic thought are brought to bear on the question of Christian theological relevance, and it is there observed that more than one of the prominent scholars in the early economics tradition explicitly recanted from Christian belief.

Chapter 5 discusses the roots of economic culture in such a way as to exhibit what is called its fivefold rootage, as it actually and historically developed independently of explicit Christian influence or control. The rootage of economic thought is found in (1) a search for a supposedly viable value-free inquiry; (2) a program of thought and analysis grounded in the assumptions of the autonomy of man as a knowing, ethical, acting agent; (3) a scheme of argument that finds its determinative presuppositions in varying forms of what is referred to as immanentism, or the claim that the central explanatory principle that guides inquiry is to be found within the universe whose explanation is sought (forms of immanentism which have determined the scope and results of economic inquiry have appeared, at various stages of development, as psychologism, materialism, historicism, technologism, and most recently a thoroughgoing logic and mathematicism); (4) an economic outcome that contributes in its own way to the general formation of a materialist existentialism; and (5) a general subscription to the assumptions of the ultimate validity and pervasiveness of the laws of chance.

In Chapter 5 also, a reasonably detailed review is given of the biblical data that bear on the formation of a scriptural rootage of economic thought. Work, property, power, distribution, equity, the status of the poor, trade, exchange, wealth, inequality, investment, and government responsibility are examined for the light that is to be brought to bear on them from biblical categories.

Chapter 6, "Economics, Culture, and Rationality," widens the discussion to a number of larger issues that come to focus in economic theory and arrangements and on which also the Scriptures throw significant light. Here a further consideration is given to the claim of early economics that it necessarily had to set out to construct a value-free inquiry. Some critical commentaries from the development of the science are discussed. In this context also, further observations are made on the possibility of the emergence of automatic harmonies in the economic system, and attention is given to the implications of the answer to that question for economic policy considerations. It is suggested that a prime source of disruption, disequilibrium, and disharmony is found in the emergence in society of excessive concentrations of economic power. The tendency emerges all too readily to exploit such concentrations of power to the disadvantage of society and the denial of maximum economic welfare and benefit. The place and significance of such power sources as government, industrial corporations, and labor unions are examined.

In the discussion of power and the clashes and antagonisms that arise from it, it is necessary to consider the claims of Marxism and its precipitate of the class struggle in society. This leads to a slightly more extended and precise consideration of the state and its economic function and prerogatives. In relation to this the prerogatives of individual property and responsibilities are underlined. Biblical data are invoked at the many critical points relevant to this analysis. Chapter 6 concludes with a brief analysis of the viewpoints on economic theory and argument presented in a recent and important work by the Christian historian and philosopher C. Gregg Singer. It is found that his analysis in the area of economics does not deserve as high praise as does his valuable work in a number of other areas.

Introduction and Reader's Guide

The final chapter draws together the threads of analysis and discusses some of the implications of the work for questions of individualism and solidarity. It examines an application of the latter to the meaning and organization of the industrial corporation. This brief discussion considers the economic relations between such "classes" as capitalists on the one hand and labor on the other, and points the way to a new understanding of cooperative and collaborative relations in business enterprise. Questions of solidarity come to expression also in relation to international poverty, economic aid, trade, and income and wealth comparisons.

The analysis concludes with a discussion of two highly significant theological categories that bring the totality of economic, theological, and cultural concerns to a sharply defined coalescence. These have to do, first, with the biblical doctrine of "common grace," and second, with the nature of the eschatological or teleological perspective from which our view of the unfolding of human affairs is commanded. The question of common grace is highly relevant to the matter of the epistemological foundations of work in economics, as in every other area of human intellection and investigative inquiry. In the early chapters of the book attention is drawn to what is there called the rationalist-irrationalist dialecticism in modern thought, meaning by that the holding in tension of competing or contradictory assumptions as to man's knowledge capacities and potential. It is on the one hand assumed that man, on the basis of his autonomous reason and rational capacities, could aspire to comprehensiveness of knowledge. On the other hand it is postulated that all eventuation in fact is governed by the pervasive laws of chance and that therefore man could, in the final analysis, know nothing at all. Comprehensiveness of knowledge resulting from autonomously interpretative inquiry, and the unknowableness of events and outcomes thrown up by randomness and chance, mark the swings of the pendulum tracing out the epistemological assumptions.

In the discussion of these foundations of knowledge in general, and of work in the economics discipline in particular, acknowledgment is made to Cornelius Van Til's summary of the matter in his book *Common Grace and the Gospel* (Phillipsburg, N.J.: Presbyterian and Reformed, 1973). He argues, with reference to the epistemological capacities and potential of the Christian believer on the one hand and the unbeliever on the other, that "metaphysically both parties have all things in common, while epistemologically they have nothing in common." The issue that arises is resolved by the realization that only those know truly, and have true knowledge of things and events and facts in all of the reality structures in which we are enmeshed, who know God truly. For then they see the facts truly as God's facts. The facts are not, in any situation or on any level of human inquiry, basic epistemological data in the sense that they are "raw" or "brute" or uninterpreted facts. The facts are what they are because they are God's facts and because they have already been thought by Him and established by Him in their apparently contingent relations. The epistemological task, therefore, is not that of man's interpreting the facts he discovers. For those facts have already been interpreted by God who established them. As Van Til has put it, the task of human knowledge and investigative processes is not to be "creatively constructive" at all, but to be "recreatively reconstructive" under God, who calls men to think His thoughts after Him.

But this does not mean that no validity or significance attaches to scientific work, in economics for example or in other natural and social sciences. For it is by the administration of His common grace that God permits and enables men, including unregenerate men and unbelievers, to make contributions to the edifice of human knowledge. He releases the forces of creative power implanted in them, and they thereby make contributions to the human awareness of truth in spite of their own mistaken principles of autonomy and their misguided epistemological stance. For the non-Christian thinker the discovery of truth is in a final sense accidental and casual, for the reality structures with which he deals are precisely the opposite of what he imagines them to be. They are in fact God's structures, and they consist and cohere in accordance with God's established relational laws. It is clearly at this point that the most important division in the

Introduction and Reader's Guide 13

entire range of philosophic presupposition exists between the Christian believer and the unbeliever. It is accordingly of considerable importance that these and other relevant issues be sorted out with some care. It is for this reason that, having introduced the matter in the initial background chapters, a fuller clarification of the kind just referred to is given at the conclusion of the work.

The final question, which again provides a determinative underpinning for the work as a whole, has to do with the eschatological perspective in terms of which one's thinking about human history in general, and the significance of economic structures in particular, proceeds. By the terms that have just been employed, reference is being made to the nature of the end or purpose to which, through the temporal process, the creation now moves. That movement, it is argued, is through an arc of divine intent and is not unidirectionally determined. Reality moves, that is, through a process of history toward what is termed a double maturation. There lies ahead a maturation of evil and a maturation of good. The time process moves on, and at the end, at the final crack of doom, both unregenerate men and God's people redeemed in Christ will have come to full epistemological self-consciousness. The one will have become finally mature in their apostasy from the obligations which God imposed upon them in His initial creation covenant, and the other will have become mature in the righteousness to which they have been introduced in Christ.

It is this realization that saves the Christian culturist from the spurious choice of either cultural optimism or cultural pessimism. For Christ is King. He is administering His kingship over a fallen world and in the hearts of fallen men through the operation of His common grace, and He will assuredly bring to pass the purposes that He has intended. The high privilege and responsibility of the Christian economist is that he is called to play a part in the realization of that very purpose, laboring by the grace of God for a nobler prize than the non-Christian enmeshed in the web of the process can even begin to imagine.

2
The Problem

A sense of confusion, futility, and escape to a cultural negativism is abroad in our time. Our higher hopes for the century of the common man have crumbled; the materialism we have worshiped has trapped us in its spiritual emptiness; and clashes of ideology have left us confused and uncertain of our prospects. In our thought constructions we have long since retreated from the larger questions of meaning and being and from the proper grasp of the ontological structure of things that lies behind our possibilities of knowing and doing. We have lowered our sights and have earth-bound our vision, and our intellectual culture has edged to a nihilism born of a Kantian disclaimer that knowledge resides or inheres anywhere but in his so-called phenomenal realm. The noumenal may be there. But the thing-in-itself is unknowable. Knowledge is abolished to make room for "faith," a faith, however, in what is beyond perception and intellection and is therefore beyond all capability of determining criteria for social and personal behavior.

In the world of thought our post-Kantian epistemologies have fathered a positivist-scientific method; and in behavior and social theory we have arrived at a substantially existentialist mysticism. The details of the movements will engage us in due course. But in the outcome, positivism has passed into linguistics, and humanism has passed into existentialism, and from all these levels, taking account of the cultural and intellectual lags that

The Problem 15

have occurred, influences have been transmitted to behavior norms and attitudes in society at large. The problem of the age, in short, if our perspective could be compressed for a moment to what itself threatens to partake of cliché, is the problem of man, of modern man enmeshed in a terribly human condition in which the individual has lost a clear view of his status and his place. In an age edging to cultural collapse, man in the large, engulfed in the clichés of a scientific humanism, has surrendered man the individual to a cipher, a digit in the ironic, dehumanized outcome that science, too large for morality, conceived. The inner logic and the gathering momentum of modern thought have fathered a new humanism, fostered by the philosophic enlightenment and the ultimately positivist and scientific methodology it implied, and have set the stage for a complete devolution of thought away from its earlier and secure moorings.

The milieu of contemporary thought and culture will be explored and connoted at more length in the following chapter. For the present, the perspective that has been opened can be expanded to observe that a legitimate humanism, if I may use language in such a way, that once studied man in a God-centered or theocentric structure of thought whose moorings were distinctively revelatory, has given way progressively over the last two hundred years to a man-centered or crassly anthropocentric humanism. And in this process we have arrived at the condition in which man now finds in himself, stultifying though the outcome of his efforts is, the principle of all his attempts at explanation. Man, in this view and in the determinative thought forms which the perspective implies, has seen himself as "the measure of all things."[1] Man has made himself the measure of all things on two levels that, taken together, are correlative to each other: first, on the level of behavior or ethics man is the measure of all things in that he sets his own standards or criteria of goodness, and in so doing loses himself in a shoreless ocean of relativism in which his structureless norms have lost all grip on an earlier ethical absolutism; and second, man has become the measure of all things on the level of the possibility and validity of knowledge.

In his epistemology, that is in his answer to the question, "How do we know?" man has established himself as the final reference point in all predication. Putting together the modern assertion of his autonomy in the areas of both ethics and epistemology, or of both behavior and knowledge, man has cut himself off completely from earlier and revelatory moorings.

Our problem, therefore, and the task before us is twofold. First, we shall endeavor to sketch, in a highly adumbrated form, the principal sociocultural, intellectual, and economic forces that have together determined the structure of the times. Second, we shall be particularly concerned with the manner in which, and the extent to which, economic thought and categories have intermeshed with other forces to determine our condition. And in examining both these aspects of the general scheme of things we shall consider the relevance, for both our cultural condition and the development of economic thought, of the determinative thought forms of Christian belief. Coming into principal focus, therefore, will be categories of Christian belief on the one hand and of economic thought on the other. In establishing this relationship, or the corresponding sets of relationships, we shall have occasion to take note of a significant body of professional economic literature that has preceded us in these fields. It will be instructive to take note of the ways in which the principal architects of the economics discipline themselves viewed the relation between their work and Christian-theological ideas or determinative viewpoints. That they were in many instances deliberately articulate on this important relationship will not only be of considerable assistance to the ongoing study, but will itself lend legitimacy to our method and conclusions at some critical points.[2]

Although we shall take particular note of both theological categories and those of economic analysis, one important disclaimer needs to be carefully observed. On the one side, we shall not set out to exhibit any extensive corpus of theological doctrine in its own right or for its own sake. Rather, we shall be concerned to establish the relevance of Christian norms as they bear, and as they have been seen by earlier economic thinkers to bear, on the

The Problem

issues of substance we shall discuss. And on the other side, we shall not exhibit any extensive scheme or system of economic analysis or details of what determines economic outcomes and the possibilities of their equilibration in society, or what, on the basis of them, might be thought to be an optimal mix of economic policies. From the sides of both Christian belief and economic thought, it will be necessary to invoke in outline the structures of analysis from which, if the tasks in hand were different, full-blown theologies and economics could be developed. But our present task is the much more modest one of constructing the outlines of what determines the position in which we stand, as the mutual relevance, the close contiguity, and the extensive interaffiliation of sociocultural, economic, and Christian thought forms are observed.

Our thesis requires the observation that we stand now at a point of confluence of sociocultural and theological issues. And that confluence, it follows from what we have already said, comes to poignant focus in the jointly determinative preoccupation of both theological and secular thought with the problem of man. We have spoken of a new scientific humanism, but it is significant that it is not universally agreed that all is well with the scientific enterprise itself or with its explanatory significance. The editors of *Time* magazine, for example, have evaluated our intellectual condition by saying (April 2, 1973):

> By whatever name, there is an impending sense of change in the world of ideas. The reigning wisdom that informed and compelled the past few decades is under attack—or, at the very least, under cross-examination. That wisdom has been variously called liberalism, rationalism, scientism. . . . But now man's confidence in his power to control his world is at a low ebb. Technology is seen as a dangerous ally, and progress is suspect. Even the evolutionists share this unease; their hope lies not in man as he is but in some mutant superman. . . . The aggressive humanism of the Renaissance and the mechanistic visions of the scientific revolution shattered [man's] unified cosmos.

Unfortunately, the forces of methodological scientism have widened the gulf between theology and philosophy over the last two hundred years. During that time theology has changed, and in the main has proceeded via a naturalistic deism to forms of subjectivism and modernism which have moved it unrecognizably away from the accomplishments, for example, of the great Reformation watershed. And philosophy has also changed. It has moved, while still remaining outside the limits of the sixteenth-century Reformation and orthodox Christian thought, away from its system building under the postulates of God, creation, and providence, via a new rationalism in the Continental philosophers Descartes, Spinoza, and Leibnitz, and a tradition of empiricism and sensationalist thought in John Locke, George Berkeley, and David Hume, to coalesce in Immanuel Kant. It moved on through forms of nineteenth-century subjectivism and idealism to reach a virtual denial of the possibility of philosophy, at least in its historic metaphysical expression. It became tied up with questions of method, logical positivism for example, and later with logic and language.

But through all these developments that changed the world runs the thread of science, and we live now at the culmination of three hundred years of the scientific age. The age of science, and its derivatives of technology and applied science in all its forms, have implied two things: first, a new view of the status and significance of man; and second, a new view of the method and validity of knowledge.

We are familiar with the modern retreat from the understanding of the dignity of man inherent in his creation in the image of his Creator, and with the embrace of probabilistic evolutionary hypotheses. Indeed, on the one hand we have the view of William Nicholls's *Systematic and Philosophical Theology* that "man now regards himself as a master of nature, as the agent of his own evolution. . . . Contemporary sensibility sees man as a part of nature. . . . It sees him as continuous with nature."[3] And on the other hand we have the editors of *Time* concluding that "at the heart of the ferment of the seventies is a deep, even humble perception that man and his universe are more complex than he recently thought. Experts are under fire, because their solutions have proven to be less certain than advertised, or because they

The Problem

have seemed to sacrifice the whole man to one of his parts." This last statement is, of course, the crucial point. The sacrifice of the whole man to one of his parts, coming into focus and expressing itself in myriad ways, will engage us at many points in the following argument.

* * *

Let us expand our background perspectives slightly in both their philosophico-theological and their economic dimensions. In doing so, we shall provide a closer preliminary look at the main framework of ideas to be considered in what follows.

The Christian church, it is all too clear, no longer enjoys a cultural hegemony or takes an influential stance in the world. We live in a secular age. It is true that the secular states, particularly those of Western society as we know it, are drawing more heavily than is acknowledged on the residue of moral capital inherited from Christianity. And it is undoubtedly true that our social and our cultural cohesion wears thin as we continue to imagine that we can support the Christian ethic while collapsing the Christian doctrine that determines it. But it is true also that we live in a pluralist society in which the church, in spite of what might have been the case in earlier centuries, has ceased culturally to be an effective and cementing establishment. We live in an age in which, such is now the radical pluralism of our society, no single force appears capable of functioning universally as an effective and culturally coordinating establishment. No single force exerts a predominant, determining influence or a cultural hegemony or leadership except the applied forms of the new humanism, particularly in its scientific and its empirical expressions.

It was not always so. In earlier times, there were "giants in the earth,"[4] and men of God stood tall, men whose beliefs harnessed their passions and nerved their energies to bequeath ongoing centuries of political, economic, and scientific development. History tells us of the definitive debate in the fourth century when Augustine laid to rest the Pelagian heresy, and of the

Reformation in the sixteenth century whose light has shattered the darkness of Europe and of the New World for some four centuries since. We know, too, of the flowering of industrial and financial capitalism since the liberating breath of a new individualism blew across Europe from the Reformation times; of the struggle for new political responsibilities and freedoms, born of a massively new theological construction by the British and American Puritans; and of these and other influences that shaped the birth and destiny of the new American states. We know, too, of the deadening hand of deism and the encroach of a new materialism as maturing economic identities clashed with evangelical revivals in eighteenth- and nineteenth-century Britain and America. History makes us conscious of the kaleidic forces that, in all these aspects of human experience and expression, converged, for good and for ill, to determine the uniqueness of our cultural and our socioeconomic heritage.

But one clear thread, a reddened strain through the fabric of four hundred years of social history, runs clear and inescapably across the years that have brought us to our present condition; to a condition of advanced capitalism and its attendant and worrying uncertainties in economics, to new disturbances of the calmer order of things in political realities, and to expressions of new priorities in social and cultural relations which eat at the foundations of older and accustomed stabilities. There runs through the last four and a half centuries an underlying commitment to theistic assumptions that determined ethical constructs and behavioral norms at large on the one hand, and unique ways of perceiving and constructing the meaning of reality on the other. But the reddened strain runs pale, and new allegiances, newer presuppositions and knowledge constructions, have grasped men's minds. We boast that we have now "come of age," and what we imagine as new liberations have placed us where we stand. Old securities have been lost, moorings have been weakened, and we wonder where the shifting sea of unsuspected uncertainties will bring us again to land. We have looked at our birthrights and have exchanged them for hopes whose certainty now evades us, and we no longer know with any conviction at

The Problem

all whether the "mess of pottage" we are getting in exchange will have any similarity to what we might once have envisioned.

Objectivity and candor, moreover, require us to observe even more closely the indictment to be placed before the church at this time. The indictment probes inevitably further than its acquiescence in certain of the tendencies in modern thought noted already. At stake, we can say, is the church's own understanding of both its evangel and its mission in the world on the one hand, and of the needs of the day for which it should recapture its calling on the other. The church, no less than the world in which it is called to minister, confronts a crisis of comprehension in which the very explanation of man stands like a riddle at the core. What, in the end, is to be said of the church, the kaleidoscope of its rationalist theological construction, its doctrineless ecumenicity, its turmoil in ecclesiastical form, and its homilectical mediocrity? Has the church not lost the battle, it is time to ask, or is it not perilously in danger of doing so simply by falling prey to some of the shallowest and most lamentable fallacies of the age—the fallacies of imagining that it could hold an evangelism or an evangelicalism without the biblical evangel; that it could effectively preach the word of life and not be careful to hold the scriptural truths in scriptural order and in scriptural proportion; that it could afford to bend to the behavior norms of the age and become careless in the handling of holy things; that it could somehow accommodate the humanism of our time, with its subjectivist, immanentistic philosophies on the one hand, and its quasi-scientific methodologies on the other, to the radicalism of scriptural diagnoses; or that doctrineless homilies could usefully replace honest exegesis and expository preaching in an age oppressed by uneven affluence and jealous of its comforts? These, no doubt, are hard questions. But the questions themselves are those whose evasion would deserve the charge of a true obscurantism and of the abdication of the church's responsibilities to the world.

Nevertheless, Christian distinctives remain, and we shall observe more closely in a moment the manner in which, consistent with our chosen level of analysis, they come insistently to focus in providing the epistemological foundations we shall need. Intellection proceeds soundly, we shall have cause to observe, only in the clear recognition that man stands derivatively, ontologically and epistemologically derivative, under his Creator, in the image of whose perfections he was originally established. Man is because God is. He knows because God has established the foundations and possibility of knowledge and has established an accordance between the structure of things on the one hand and the cognitive capacities of man as a knowing subject on the other. Man speaks because of the fact that God has spoken. Untouched by the sorry fact that sin has entered the world, and brought to only a starker significance by the noetic effects of Adam's fall, are the determinative dimensions of the Creator-creature distinction that undergirds the entire process of human knowledge, as it does the awareness of personal identity and the validity of self-identification.

A further point also gives scope to our analysis. This is the fact that uniquely at the present time both Christian thought and the discipline of economics that undergirds our analysis of society are incomplete. They are incomplete in a sense that has not been the case at earlier points of their history. We have spoken already of the apologetic and philosophic accommodations that the theology of the church has made with the tenor of the times. There are "tensions in contemporary theology," and searches are under way for new options in belief.[5] We shall not expand the argument at this time. But it is equally the case that this conviction of incompleteness, the air of having in a sense lost its way, is all too clearly present in the discipline of economics also. Economics as an intellectual discipline is suddenly not so sure of itself, and its empirical relevance and prescriptive competence are called increasingly in question.

The outlines of this discontent are clear on only a minimal inspection. An earlier and comfortable orthodoxy has been shattered, and new ways of looking at the world are being sought to repair the logical inadequacies and the empirical irrelevancies of economic science. Assumptions that the economic world was continually in some kind of describable equilibrium; that automatic harmonies existed and propelled the economy continually

The Problem

to positions of maximum benefit and welfare; that simplistic analyses that abstracted from the dynamics of real historic time could adequately explain observable states of affairs; that labor and capital were in a simple sense coordinate factors of production, the explanation of whose employment and rewards was amenable to treatment by a common theoretical model—these comfortable simplicities, these damaging illusions we might say, have been fairly completely shattered, and new paradigms of economic argument have emerged. The assumptions of equilibrium, of the presence in the economic system of so-called "risks" that could be assumed away by the application of a calculus of probability based on postulates of randomness and chance, of the safety in analysis of ignoring genuine time, have had to give way to newer perspectives. An earlier crust of orthodoxy has crumbled. New examinations of disequilibrium as opposed to equilibrium have emerged, considerations of genuine or residual uncertainty have replaced the easy assumptions of controllable risk, and improved methods of handling the meaning of time, historic, unidirectional, and irreversible as opposed to logical time, have appeared.[6]

We shall see in particular, as our economic analysis and Christian categories of thought are brought closer together, that a critically damaging assumption of the older economics was that of the presence of automatic harmonies in the system. It was assumed, in other words, that if left to itself the economic system would automatically tend to generate that level of activity which would provide employment and maximum economic welfare for all those seeking to work, and that a freely functioning enterprise market system would best guarantee long-run stability and economic growth. It is a pity that in some of their most articulate economic criticism at this time some spokesmen for the Christian church have remained wedded to the intellectually empty and ethically defective assumptions of automatic harmonies. Surely if nothing else had been perceived, it should have been observed that the very essence of Christian dogma, the fact that sin is abroad in the world and in the hearts of men, would give the lie to an easy reliance on the harmony postulates.[7]

We shall probe these implications further. For the present, it is of correlative importance to note, at least in a similarly adumbrated form, what might be characterized as the modern intellectual tradition against which both the stance of Christianity in the world and the issues of our cultural condition and our "affluent society"[8] can be examined.

* * *

We shall refer in what follows to what can be called the essential dialectical feature of contemporary thought. We have chosen this descriptive phrase for its hopefully explanatory significance. For it is in the dialectical nature of modern thought, by which we mean a shifting back and forth, a swinging to and fro, between one type or character of explanatory principle and another, the latter in essence the opposite or contradiction of the former, that the modern position is essentially characterized. It is this shifting of ground, this successive emergence and alternating recognition of the logical implications of the ground and starting point on which modern man stands, that we refer to as a dialecticism. It is not simply that the modern journey into knowledge is thereby guilty of false starts, new beginnings, and changing directions. The issue of dialecticism needs to be recognized on a somewhat deeper level of logic and significance. It is endemic in non-Christian thought, naturally present, unavoidably a part of its very fabric, that the opposing or contradictory principles that might thus be adduced are each legitimately features of the thought schemes in view. By the dialecticism of the age we mean this essential, this logically unavoidable characterization of its explanatory constructs by what is, on one view, an internal contradiction, an emergence of mutually incompatible explanatory principles, but is, on another view, a true and even a necessary feature and description of the state of affairs.

It is not that modern non-Christian thought is necessarily guilty of misusing the rules of logic or offending against the laws of the syllogism. It is not that the rules of the syllogism are different for Christians and non-Christians. A distinction exists, rather, at the level of the initial, the foundational, the fundamental deter-

The Problem

minative starting point of the logical or the epistemological journey. The dialecticism of modern thought can be characterized by referring to what we shall label the non-Christian principle of continuity on the one hand, and a corresponding principle of discontinuity on the other.[9]

The former principle implies that on the metaphysical level there exists the notion of being-in-general in which man and God, if He exists at all, both participate. And on the epistemological level it implies the correlative notion that there exists a universal or generalized reason, essentially penetrable to the human mind, in which again man and God, if He exists, both participate. Modern thought, therefore, and in general, has suppressed the essential determinative postulate of Christian thought, namely the fact of a Creator-creature distinction on both the metaphysical and epistemological levels. The modern epistemological assumption implies the postulate that what is knowable to man is, given only time and resources, knowable completely. Raised at the beginning of the knowledge and explanatory process is the vision and assumption of comprehensiveness, or completeness in knowledge. Man is said to have known truly when he has known comprehensively and exhaustively.

But over against this principle of continuity is the alternative postulate, equally present, pervasively and coordinately determinative, the non-Christian principle of discontinuity. This principle, essentially, involves the assumption of the noncreatedness of the universe and the operation of chance, randomness, and stochastic or probabilistic laws underlying all things. This principle of discontinuity, in short, involves the assumption of the ultimacy of chance. Anything can happen. When Shakespeare said, "There's a divinity that shapes our ends, rough-hew them how we will,"[10] he was putting together attractive iambics, but he was saying nothing at all of substance.

The important point is that in this basic dialecticism, the first assumption we raised, that of continuity and reason-in-general, stamps modern thought with its aspect of rationalism. The second assumption, that of discontinuity or the ultimacy of chance, stamps it with its aspect of irrationalism. And this, in short, exhibits the rationalist-irrationalist dialectic of the age. It implies that against the earlier implicit assumption of exhaustiveness or comprehensiveness of knowledge we must place the equally pervasive assumption that at the end of all his investigative processes man can know nothing at all. All is chance. This, in a sentence, is, on the epistemological level, the dilemma of modern thought. Man either knows everything or he knows nothing. It will be useful to note briefly one stark example of the antithetical thought systems now in view.

The Christian's escape from this modern dialecticism results from his acknowledgment that the reference point in all of his predication of meaning is found in God and His plan, mediated and declared to men in Jesus Christ His Son. All the facts of created reality, the Christian acknowledges, are God's facts, and all the coherences and constellations of facts are what they are because of the place they occupy in the plan of God. Given the revelation of God in Christ, which has for two millennia "turned the world upside down"[11] and left untouched none of the histories of nations and men, the Christian sees that all of the facts of his environment must be Christologically interpreted. They are what they are because they are placed where they are in the unfolding of human history. This points to the final and eschatological denouement, when "in the dispensation of the fullness of times" God will again "gather together in one all things in Christ."[12] It is this interpretative standpoint that is, for Christian thought, its basic epistemological presupposition, or is, because of its revelatory character, the foundational epistemological datum.

Against this view let us consider, to take only one example from economic work, an argument by the distinguished Cambridge economist D. G. Champernowne in his *Uncertainty and Estimation in Economics*.[13] At the beginning of his work, in the course of laying the conceptual and philosophical foundations of his subject, Champernowne discusses the notion of "irrelevance" between independent events, referring to it as "about the most fundamental concept in the whole theory of probability." In this context he illustrates the nature of his conceptualization in a

The Problem

somewhat startling fashion by stating that "whether Christ ascended into heaven is irrelevant to whether this fair coin will come down heads or tails."[14]

To focus on the only point in this statement that is at issue at present, it may appear that the instance is minute, even trivial, hardly adequate to bear whatever philosophical weight might be placed upon it. But on the contrary, the very appearance of triviality can itself bring into focus the important and underlying postulates we are concerned with. For if, as has just been argued, every fact in the universe must be Christologically interpreted, the question now before us is rescued from the frivolous by the enormity of its potential relevance. Is, or is not, we can ask, the fact of Christ's ascension, and therefore His finished work in this world, relevant to Champernowne's problem? To press the issue, is it of any significance to say that the apparently random outcome of tossing a coin can have any conceivable relation to the work of Christ?

Before we answer this question in the affirmative, let us acknowledge what would be the implication if it were to be answered in the negative. This would mean that, contrary to the underlying postulate of Christian thought, we had actually discovered one fact situation to which the work of Christ had no relevance. Our basic epistemological postulate would then be punctured. And if there is one point in the phenomenal universe at which the work of Christ is acknowledged not to have significance, then conceivably other such points are also discoverable. The question is then presented of where in fact the so-called cosmic significance of Christ does begin to take effect. If the work of Christ is irrelevant to any fact, it is conceivably irrelevant to all.

The question before us in this seemingly inconsequential case in hand demands an affirmative answer, therefore, for a threefold reason. First, God, the Christian has posited, is the *author of possibility,* and the outcome of all things and events is dependent upon His sovereign plan and His sovereign ordering. Second, to argue to the contrary would imply that there existed, or existed potentially in the universe, a fact situation, seemingly inconsequential though it may be, which God had not ordered and of which He accordingly had no anterior cognizance. In that case, God would have to wait to discover the outcome of an intramundane event, and this, it will be clear, is to introduce a temporal successiveness into the knowledge of God. This, in turn, is tantamount to the introduction of temporal succession into the being of God, or into His knowledge of Himself. God is in that case no longer the sovereign God of the Scriptures, self-existent beyond the temporal process He has created. On the contrary, it has been claimed, God's knowledge of the facts exists by virtue of His having thought all the facts and ordered them in their apparently contingent relations. Third, it is in Christ and by virtue of His work that God accomplishes His plan and His ordering of all of the affairs of all that He has made. It would then be taxing credulity to imagine that the work of Christ, who Himself has said, "Are not two sparrows sold for a farthing? and not one of them shall fall on the ground without your Father. But the very hairs of your head are all numbered" (Matt. 10:29), should be irrelevant to the outcome of Champernowne's toss of a coin. For who is to say, in the interdependent and causal nexus of events, what issues of larger enormity might follow from the tossing of the coin?

* * *

Our perspective on economics as a distinguishable intellectual discipline finds the formative principle, or the coordinating concept with which the study of economics can be approached, in the notion of *conservation*. By this we mean that the economic problem is that of conserving the social environment of potentially need-satisfying resources and using them or transforming them into social satisfactions in such a way as to achieve a maximum benefit for the members of the society or race or human population in view. This notion, although it begs completely at this stage the question of the appropriate criteria of need specification and need satisfaction, does point to a wider connotation of economics than is normally implicit in the indi-

The Problem

vidualist, hedonist, "utility" optimizing calculus of the neoclassical tradition in the discipline. This notion of conservation, moreover, imports into economic discussion an important correlative idea that needs also to inform any thoroughgoing critique of our economic problem, particularly as that critique comes from the direction of Christian perspectives. This is the idea, or category, of *stewardship,* meaning thereby that there exists a basic moral and ethical responsibility for right behavior in the use and allocation of resources over which we have control at any time. Conservation, in correlation with stewardship, lies at the heart of the economic question and the understanding of it as a part of our larger cultural position.

It is in the initial creation mandate that responsible stewardship over the need-satisfying resources inherent in created reality is established: "So God created man in his own image.... And God blessed them, and God said unto them, Be fruitful and multiply, and replenish the earth, and subdue it: and have dominion over . . . every living thing" (Gen. 1:27-28). In this, man is established in his original constitution in terms of a covenant relation to his Creator-God, sustaining a responsibility for the administration to the glory of God of the resources over which he was thus given a delegated authority. To say this, however, or to say that man exists createdly and derivatively and not autonomously, and to say that he thus acquired authority and governing prerogatives derivatively, points immediately to a widening of the categories of economic interpretation. It thereby becomes imperative to avoid the tendency to equate the legitimate limits of economic objectives and behavior with the narrowly defined interests of atomistic, personal, individualistic satisfactions. For in this latter direction lies the betrayal of the larger questions of genuine human and social obligations. Economics thus conceived is all too quickly in danger of being trapped in the fruitless morass of anarchies, exploitation, and societal disharmonies.

This, of course, is to say that economics is not and cannot be a value-free inquiry. On one level our economic thought and prescriptions are dependent on the philosophic structures embedded in our consciousness, our life view, and our cultural *Weltanschauung*. But it should be equally clear that the value alternatives that claim consideration depend on larger, or deeper, categories than those which many of the common arguments regarding economic structures envisage. Economic inquiry is not exhausted, for example, and its limits are not properly defined, by arguments for the priority of individualism, socialism, laissez-faire capitalism, or collectivism. For underlying the interesting and important capitalism-socialism and collectivism-individualism dichotomies there reside deeper springs and motivations of human action. And it is these latter that must necessarily come into focus if adequate account is to be taken of the stewardship and correlative responsibilities already noted.

It is true that both the subject matter of economic inquiry and its methods of analysis owed much throughout their development in the nineteenth century to the optimistic humanism that glowed in Victorian England, though significant substreams of dissent and stirrings of social conscience were also to be found. At the present time, when the pervasive relevance of a measurable, quantifiable, positivist economics is being increasingly called in question, both the legitimate substance of economics and its methods of inquiry are in a state of uncertainty and flux. The euphoria of mid-twentieth-century prosperity, of high rates of economic growth and an increasing abundance of material things, has begun to generate a new economic conscience. Suddenly, doubts are rising about the rightness of the distribution of the benefits of economic development and the sharing of the fruits of economic growth. Some people in some places—too many, some economists are beginning to think—are still too hungry, and too few have too much of what the economic machine has produced. Materialism exposes an emptiness that is embarrassing because it exposes the futility of much of our cultural and economic endeavor. Resources and endowments, as well as people and societies, have been seen to be exploited, and the pollution and destruction of ecological health that economic progress has demanded have suddenly seemed a high price to pay.

This crystallization of the formative principle of economics

The Problem

under the heading of conservation will be expanded in what follows to embrace two further and cognate categories. We shall refer to these as *development,* on the one hand, and *equity,* on the other. And in terms of these three determinative ideas—conservation, development, and equity—the questions of economics and economic behavior can be accorded an adequately full treatment. These categories inhere, it will be seen, in what we have already referred to as the creation mandate, which established man in responsible stewardship over the resources of his environment in the first place. And we have already implied that in examining the applicability of these categories, account must be taken not only of man's creaturehood status and the derivative responsibilities that that implies, but also of the fact of sin. It is this fact that lies at the heart not only of Judeo-Christian thought systems and ethics, but at the heart also, even if only by a dimly articulated awareness, of the last four hundred years of the Western societies' economic, industrial, and political development. We have said already that though the residue of moral capital inherited from Christianity is there in society to be seen, it now wears thin, and the question remaining is undoubtedly that of the length of time for which the social ethic it has supported can continue without the Christian doctrine that previously sustained it. No point can be served by avoiding the implications of these terms. For life is religious in the sense that human action necessarily moves within the orbit of response to the *sensus deitatis,* the awareness of God, from which the human consciousness cannot voluntarily escape. Life structures are then, in the very nature of the case, necessarily directed toward, or away from, the source of meaning which the status of creaturehood implies.

But Christian thought does not suppose that the formative principle of economics inheres primarily in human sin. It inheres not in our sin but in our finitude, functioning as we do within the framework of a similarly created temporal process. Sin, of course, has determined the *form* of all subsequent economic activity. But the *fact* and the existence of an economic problem, the existence, that is, of the economic dimension of reality, quite apart from the form in which it has come to expression in the events that followed from "man's first disobedience,"[15] are embedded in our finitude. We shall return to the point.

For the present, we can observe that it is in this way that our abundant society stands, because man himself and his categories of understanding and behavior stand, under God and in responsible relation to Him. The questions before us now have to do with the cultural and socioeconomic structures that inhere in the scheme of things, the categories determining their qualities of rightness or wrongness, and the instabilities and inequities that occur within them. We shall be concerned also with the manner in which those structures themselves might more completely accord, along with the actions of individuals within them, with the canons of ethics inherent in the interpretative standpoint that Christian analysis suggests.

3

The Intellectual—Cultural Condition

In the preceding chapter we have observed, though at this stage in an outline and highly summarized form, some of the principal categories our analysis has in view. Substantially, our concern turns on three points: first, the development of the intellectual-cultural tradition that has landed us in a pervasive existentialism or, on the level of thought, in what we have termed a rationalist-irrationalist dialecticism; second, the nature of the emerging and sharply changing traditions in economic thought that have also contributed to our social condition; and third, the contiguity, and the intermeshing and interdependent significance for these developments, of traditions in Christian belief. In the next three chapters, we shall look in more detail at these three points of orientation or concern.

Protagoras, the Greek philosopher of the fifth pre-Christian century, crystallized the thrust of apostate thought in his dictum that "man is the measure of all things." The remarkable feature of the history of thought is its consistency, not of achievement, but of substantial commitment to the early Protagorean premise. In the earlier Christian period this continued to be the case. It came to expression in the Pelagian emphasis on human ability in its controversy in the fifth century with the Augustinian insistence on divine grace; and it reappeared in the massive philosophico-theological achievement of Thomas Aquinas in the thirteenth century, when his defective anthropology stemming from a low view of sin and the fall permitted the importation to theology of the classical Aristotelian philosophy. On through the Renaissance that spread from the thirteenth to the fifteenth centuries in Europe, through the repetition of the Pelagian-Augustinian controversy in the debates between Erasmus and Luther, or Pighius and Calvin, in the sixteenth century, and between the Arminians and the more orthodox authors of the Canons of Dort in the seventeenth century, scriptural and theological orthodoxy contended repeatedly with countersystems whose genesis and genius stemmed from an elevated view of man.

It is as though the eighteenth-century poet Alexander Pope had caught the tenor of the times. Having condensed in his couplet the meaning of the Enlightenment age of which he was the child, he thrust its message forward to Kant and his offspring in the following century, to the positivism of the twentieth century, and to the modern systems based on the postulate of autonomous man. In the peroration of his *Essay on Man,* Pope had written, "Know then thyself, presume not God to scan; the proper study of mankind is man." Pope's "know thyself" harks back to the same injunction of Socrates and is potentially as empty of meaning as every system that turns its back on the scriptural claim: "In Christ are hid all the treasures of wisdom and knowledge" (Col. 2:3). "The proper study of mankind" that Pope enjoined became the religion of the Enlightenment age, and its essential articles are adequately summarized by Carl Becker in his *The Heavenly City of the Eighteenth-Century Philosophers:* "(1) Man is not natively depraved; (2) the end of life is life itself, the good life on earth instead of the beatific life after death; (3) man is capable, guided solely by the light of reason and experience, of perfecting the good life on earth; and (4) the first and essential condition of the good life on earth is the freeing of men's minds from the bonds of ignorance and superstition."[1]

The optimistic humanism that glows in prescriptions such as these, an optimism that came to a peculiarly confident expression as the twentieth century dawned, has in more recent decades been severely shaken. And no doubt the old faith in its old form is not as widely or as expectantly embraced. In an acute sense a philosophy of negation, of nihilism and despair, has taken the place of the humanist faith of earlier times. Existentialism, more frequently an attitude and an individualistic stance against the world than a philosophic system, has replaced the happier and rationalistic humanism of the last century. The nerve centers of the new attitude are disclosed by H. B. Acton's summary:

> The word [existence] is then used to emphasize the claim that each individual person is unique in terms of any metaphysical or scientific system; that he is a being who chooses as well as a being who thinks or contemplates; that he is free and that, because he is free, he suffers; and that since his future depends in part upon his free choices it is not altogether predictable. . . . Running through all these different though connected suggestions is the fundamental idea that each person exists and chooses in time and has only a limited amount of it at his disposal in which to make decisions which matter so much to him. Time is short; there are urgent decisions to take; we are free to take them, but the thought of how much depends upon our decision makes our freedom a source of anguish, for we cannot know with any certainty what will become of us.[2]

Existentialism, in its secular expression and in what has become its militantly atheistic form, has elevated to unique focus this multifaceted question of individual personal existence. Colin Brown has correctly and briefly summed up the meaning of this for Sartre, for example, the French existentialist:

> Man is dumped into the world. Whether he likes it or not, he must fend for himself. He must work out his own values. He cannot avoid making choices. Even when he tries to put off a choice, that in itself is an act of choice. And what he chooses all contributes towards making him the kind of person he is becoming. Man's nature is never fixed at any time. It is always the product of what he does, thinks, and chooses.

And all the time hanging over him is the prospect of death and the anxieties which are part and parcel of his lonely existence. Man is right to pursue high ideals, but death mocks everything and in the end brings everything to nothing.[3]

No doubt existentialist thought does give us some significant insights into human behavior. But it becomes clear from even a brief acquaintance with its authors that a tension exists between the demands of a well-articulated meaning-system on the one hand, and a more intensely personal, even anguished, plea and rebellion against the world and existence on the other.

The problem of man in the world, this tension implies, is acutely the problem of finding the meaning of himself and his orientation against the forces, the various social, spiritual, and material forces seemingly so clearly ranged against him. It is this crisis of meaning that gives the issue a unique coalescence with that of the church, as we have noted already. In other terms, if a single phrase were taken to sum up the condition, we exist now in an attitude and a stance that we shall refer to as "subjectivist-mystic" in its principal orientation. I have coined this phrase "subjectivist-mystic" as a means of bringing into sharper relief the two contributing strands of thought and attitude that have made the present intellectual and cultural climate what it is.

As for the subjectivist aspect, Descartes in the first post-Reformation century set the anthropocentric mold with his "cogito ergo sum," "I think therefore I am." And the influence of the philosopher Sören Kierkegaard, whose early nineteenth-century existentialism rebelled against the classic idealism which the line of rationalism from Descartes, Kant, and Hegel had fathered, constructed a new and philosophically subjective basis for Christianity. Further, the "consciousness theology" emanating from Friedrich Schleiermacher's *The Christian Faith*,[4] with its emphasis and orientation on the interpretative significance of subjective religious experience, has consolidated the groundwork on which contemporary theology rests.

Of equal importance, or of even more pressing significance in view of its relevance to the times, is the mystic element in our "subjectivist-mystic" characterization of the age. Mysticism, of course, is a natural offspring of subjectivism in its various forms. The existentialist philosophy of despair and negation traces to Kierkegaard in both its secular and theological forms. In the former expression it emerges in the work of Sartre and Camus in France, Jaspers in Switzerland, and Heidegger in Germany in the present century; and in its theological form it appears in Rudolf Bultmann in Germany, Paul Tillich in the United States, and in the writings of the contemporary theologian John Macquarrie. The latter's *Principles of Christian Theology*[5] explicitly acknowledges its indebtedness to, and dependence upon, Heidegger for "the philosophical categories employed."[6]

For this mystic aspect of our "subjectivist-mystic" characterization, it is of immediate relevance to notice two broad levels of expression. One has to do with the matter of morality and behavior, and the other with the numbness and lostness that contemporary man feels in the face of the scientific, technological, and economic pressures of the time. It will be useful to consider the latter of these aspects first.

The Christian church faces the problems that arise in this respect on at least three separate but interrelated levels. First, the church needs to be intelligently aware of the secular forces— industrial, economic, technological, political, and bureaucratic— that structure modern society. For existentialism as the root philosophy of the time is a revolt and a protest against the massness and the impersonality of this modern society. Second, the church confronts continually the question of what, if anything, should be the proper form of its participation in society; meaning by that the question of its direct participation in political processes and its involvement in the various forms and works of social amelioration. An acute tension no doubt arises in the church between a primary fidelity to the apostolic injunction to "preach the word" (II Tim. 4:2) and the pressures to excessive involvement in the pragmatics of a "social gospel." Third, the church needs to be alertly conscious of the state and condition, the attitudes and aspirations of people, as these are conditioned and circumscribed by these same societal structures. It follows, therefore, that the church faces, as has always been the case, the problem and question of communication to the world. It is for this reason that the philosophic and cultural pressures determining the age cry out for understanding, that the church might properly present its message of hope, and that men might see their true condition and the way of rescue and relief in Christ.

The manner in which the church responds to these issues, and the extent to which the purity of its doctrine and the integrity of its mission are preserved, determine its relevance to the world. If the church no longer understands the condition of man, if it has evaded the scriptural diagnosis in favor of an alternative pseudo-relevance, then its genuine relevance to the times is destroyed and it no longer has anything at all of interest or significance to say. The day no longer exists, of course, when the church provides what we called in the introduction a cultural hegemony or leadership. It is not necessary to adopt the clichés that speak of the present as a post-Christian age. For it would betray a false understanding of history and of the church to claim that a uniquely Christian age has ever existed. But the point at issue is to a large degree well taken. The church now finds itself a largely despised element in a societal complex in which, when it is not despised for its meanness, it is ignored for its irrelevance. But the sadness of the case is that at the very time when the church is thus tortured by its irrelevance and strangled by its impotence, man is crying out in his existential despair for meaning and light and hope.

We have said that the second level on which the pressures to existential despair come to expression is that of morality and behavior. The issues that cause concern on this level are so starkly and so pervasively before us that not only is an extended discussion of them rendered unnecessary, but an elaboration of the state of affairs could quickly become trite and commonplace. No doubt a sense of history alerts us to the fact that the behavior norms of the world have always stemmed from a foundation in morality antithetical to scriptural and orthodox ecclesiastical criteria. One has only to think, for example, of J. Wesley Bready's *England: Before and After Wesley*[7] and its brilliant examination of the social conditions in the eighteenth century to understand that Christians, as it is said of Lot (II Peter 2:8), have always "vexed their souls" at the condition and "conversation of the wicked." But in this time, not only have new dimensions been added in the world to the rampant immorality that abounds, but men in the name of the church have scuttled the absolutism of ethical norms to the embrace of a situational ethical relativism. The situation ethics of Joseph Fletcher[8] is only one of the most prominent of a long line of attempts by churchmen at ethical reinterpretations.

But the principal point at issue on this level goes even deeper. It is not necessary to recount the crime, the drug traffic among our children as well as adults, the prostitution thinly veiled if not paraded in any significant city, the infidelities, the tax evasions, and the thousands of cumulated dishonesties. It is not necessary to indulge in any extended argument in these respects, already well documented in other places for easy inspection, to grasp the really critical point at issue. This, quite simply, is that the moral standards of the time and the behavioral characteristics they imply are inevitably what they are because, to put it initially on the lowest level, the intellectual and philosophic commitment is what it is. As being is prior to knowledge, ontology prior to epistemology, or, to invert the order but not the substance of the argument, as the possibility as well as the content of knowledge depends upon the prior existence, being, plan, and interpretative communication of God, so the content of ethics and the structure of behavioral norms follow for the Christian from the anterior fact that God is and that He has spoken His precepts definitively. But it follows that an inversion of this relational order must with equal necessity obtain for the non-Christian. For him, his ethics shift with the relativism and introspection of his subjective and structureless norms, and he mistakenly imagines that he knows what he knows because he has autonomously imposed his own categories of interpretation on the raw phenomena of the world. His god is a deified projection of an imagined construct made in his own image.

This has implied and given rise to a mystical element in what we have referred to as the "subjectivist-mystic" characterization of the times. The end result of the intrapersonal philosophizing and the subjective experiential theologizing has been a large-scale lapse into mysticism in belief and in fact. The beginning point of explanation and the vindication and motivation of doing is found increasingly in a nonrationalized, introspective, and intrapersonal locus. In professional psychology, behaviorism and Freudianism, which tended to look on man "as a system of psycho-physical stresses and strains without any free and responsible centre of integrity,"[9] have now looked for an internal motivating self, guided by a loose but still atheological concept of the uniqueness of the personal being. It is this introspective subjectivity, coming to expression in various ways in the areas we have touched, structureless, pseudo-free, unaccountable, and tenaciously individualistic, that we have labeled the mystical element in our subjectivist-mystic characterization.

* * *

The aspect of irrationalism in what we have termed the rationalist-irrationalist dialecticism stems, we have said, from the atheological-epistemological postulate of the ultimacy of chance. There do occur, of course, cultural and articulation lags between the intelligentsia and the formulators of philosophic fashions and cultural norms on the one hand, and the societal mass immersed in the day-to-day crushes of living on the other. Whether the humanist, scientific, or existentialist thought forms and methodological prescriptions are at issue, the lag between the makers of opinion and the people who live out the actual form of the age is always critically real, and an evaluation of the times from the perspectives we have raised would be delinquent if it did not consciously take account of it. Take, for example, an instance of the phenomenon we have referred to.

The philosophy of logical positivism, with its formative principle of the law of verifiability and its restriction of knowledge, following Kant, to the realm of the phenomenal, has given way to an aftermath of linguistic analysis. Language and logic have lowered the sights of philosophers from the more ambitious system building of earlier times. But the point at issue is that although this is so, the methodologies implicit in positivism, the

The Intellectual–Cultural Condition 41

hypothesis testing and statistical procedures and the meaning-potential of what Karl Popper the British philosopher-logician has called the hypothetico-deductive method, along with its locking in to probabilistic assumptions and stochastic analyses, still determine the formulation and practice of the scientific method.[10] And these methodological precipitates of positivism determine the assumed explanatory significance of the same procedures as they are imported increasingly, and in increasingly mathematized forms, from the natural and physical to the social and behavioral sciences.

Other instances of the lag we have envisaged between concept formation and cultural existence are capable of occurring a little further back in the chain of relationships. The shifting fashions of thought, or even the seemingly wholesale earth movements that occur to shift dramatically the ground on which scholarship stands, frequently reverberate only slowly through the various dependent disciplines. At such times, impatience can occur in the commentators' evaluation of the state of affairs, and this year's comment on last year's fashion can be otiose by virtue of still newer metamorphoses of thought.[11] Of course, the lags between mutually relevant areas of scholarship vary in length and significance. But they inevitably occur, and they give rise to changing fashions and changing assumptions of authority.[12]

This assists us to see in sharp relief the second of the two levels on which the individualist-existentialist pattern of the times is relevant for our present discussion. This level has to do with what is, in a sense, the negative proposition that our socio-cultural analysis should avoid an exclusive commitment to any of the changing aspects and shifting tides of thought. For though it is true that an optimistic humanism has moved into existentialism, and positivism has moved into linguistics, these very phenomena are themselves to be seen as the marks traced out by the swinging pendulum of apostate man's unalterable search for the locus of meaning in himself and in his own autonomous and determinative thought forms. The same autonomously human and anthropocentric, introspective categories come into focus repeatedly in man's attempted displacement of his Creator-God, and His plan fulfilled in Christ, as the valid locus of meaning and interpretation.

It is this therefore that gives us a primary perspective in our ongoing analysis. There are, at rock bottom, just two kinds of men. There are those who say with the poet William Henley, "I am the master of my fate: I am the captain of my soul," and there are those who say with Jeremiah the prophet, "O Lord, I know that the way of man is not in himself: it is not in man that walketh to direct his steps" (Jer. 10:23). But the implication of this distinction is that it touches vitally our attitude to the whole possibility and validity and the scope and meaning of the knowledge process. The issue before us could not well be put more concisely and informatively than in Abraham Kuyper's important *Principles of Sacred Theology,* in his discussion of "the twofold development of science":

> We speak none too emphatically, therefore, when we speak of two kinds of people. Both are human, but one is inwardly different from the other, and consequently feels a different content rising from his consciousness; thus they face the cosmos from different points of view, and are impelled by different impulses. And the fact that there are two kinds of *people* occasions of necessity the fact of two kinds of human *life* and *consciousness* of life, and of two kinds of *science;* for which reason the idea of the *unity of science,* taken in its absolute sense, implies the denial of the fact of palingenesis, and therefore from principle leads to the rejection of the Christian religion.[13]

What Kuyper is implying in this statement is that in the matter of knowledge, or in the very matter of possibility and in the possibility of the identification of any fact or truth in the phenomenal world, it is not legitimately possible to appeal to any principle that is higher than the plan and counsel of God. This is simply a restatement of the orthodox theological dogma to be placed against the contemporary epistemological constructions we have already noted. "The idea of possibility," Van Til argues, "is wholly subject to the self-contained God of Scripture."[14] The phenomena that Kuyper has brought into focus, therefore, the

The Intellectual–Cultural Condition

palingenesis and its significance for knowing, are similarly at the heart of Van Til's conclusion in his *Common Grace* that, with reference to "the believer and the non-believer, . . . metaphysically both parties have all things in common while epistemologically they have nothing in common."[15] The fact situations are common for all men. But the interpretative procedures, and the grounds in which meaning-potential and cognitive significance are understood to inhere, are radically different.

The distinction is illumined also by the argument of the first chapter of John Calvin's *Institutes,* quoting here from the Beveridge translation:

> Our wisdom, in so far as it ought to be deemed true and solid wisdom, consists almost entirely of two parts: the knowledge of God and of ourselves. . . . In the first place, no man can survey himself without forthwith turning his thoughts towards the God in whom he lives and moves. . . . It is evident that man never attains to a true self-knowledge until he has previously contemplated the face of God, and come down after such contemplation to look into himself. . . . Though the knowledge of God and the knowledge of ourselves are bound together by a mutual tie, due arrangement requires that we treat of the former in the first place, and then descend to the latter.[16]

In the act of self-awareness, it is being said, man is aware of God. And this primary existential and experiential datum is seen as the beginning of every human knowledge and investigative process.

In his four-volume work, *A New Critique of Theoretical Thought,*[17] Herman Dooyeweerd has done perhaps more on a grander scale than any other Christian philosopher to demonstrate what he sees as the bankruptcy of non-Christian or, as he calls them, immanentistic philosophies. The description of "immanentistic" is accorded all those philosophical systems whose point of central or coordinating conceptualization is found somewhere within the created universe or in observable reality and its assumed coherences or in man himself. Psychologism, for example, or mathematicism, or materialism, personalism, socialism, or historicism are instances of the ways in which immanentistic philosophy has absolutized a part or aspect of man and his experience of the world and has elevated it to become the essential and determinative thought form of the system. This absolutization of a part of man and his experience, and the assumption that the part could be made exhaustively to account for the whole, is an example of what we saw in the preceding chapter as a recent concern of the editors of *Time* magazine in their characterization of the contemporary intellectual condition. The "experts are under fire," they concluded, "because they seemed to sacrifice the whole man to one of his parts."

* * *

A significant aspect of the methodological deposit of post-Kantian and Comtean positivism is found in the so-called scientific method, closely akin to what we noted above as Popper's hypothetico-deductive procedures. We can consider this in the light of what we referred to earlier as the ultimacy of the laws of chance. We have already seen an example of the thought systems at work in the reference in the preceding chapter to Champernowne's coin-tossing experiment.

The essence of the scientific method, as that finds application not only in the natural and physical but also in the social and behavioral sciences, is that of the successive and repeated testing of the scientist's hypotheses, or provisional or tentative explanations, against the facts and observable phenomena of the world. We shall leave for the present the question of the logical or existential status of the facts, or what Dooyeweerd refers to as "naive experience,"[18] and shall return later to important questions on that level. For the present, the important point is that the scientific method stemming in more or less extreme forms from the philosophy of positivism, proceeds, if we may summarize severely, through the following stages: (1) the awareness of a problem or phenomena nexus requiring explanation, (2) the formulation of a hypothesis directed tentatively toward its explanation, followed conceivably, preparatory to empirical testing, by deductive implications drawn from the hypothesis, and (3) the testing, frequently by more or less sophisticated statistical procedures, of the hypothesis against the facts. But the important point in this scientific journey is precisely the logical status of the hypothesis itself.

The hypothesis, it will be recalled, is submitted to the facts as a tentative explanation. We might ask the question, then, whether the hypothesis can conceivably be disproved. The answer is undoubtedly yes. For if the facts, or any of the facts, do not accord sufficiently closely with the hypothesis, then it and its tentative explanation must be discarded and an alternative invented and provisionally established in its place. A single observation, it is worthy of note—given that it does not accord sufficiently closely with the assumed hypothesis explaining the state of affairs—is sufficient to disprove a hypothesis. But granted, then, that a scientific hypothesis might thus be disproved, we might ask the question also whether a hypothesis can be proved. In this case the answer, equally clearly if somewhat startlingly, is no. For supposing, as a result of the procedures just envisaged, that the facts support the hypothesis, the most that can be said is that the hypothesis is thereby and to that extent confirmed, not that it has been in any sense proved. In actual fact, therefore, the objective of science is not to prove anything at all. Its objective is to disprove, and so long as provisional explanations continue to be confirmed by the facts and not disproved, they will continue to stand, or will be replaced only by more general explanations in which the previous hypotheses are subsumed as special cases. The true man of science therefore is properly a man of doubt. He disproves, but he never proves. It would take us too far afield to adduce examples of the way in which, for this reason, so-called revolutions in science and scientific explanations have occurred from time to time. It might be added, to take only one case, that the single most important example of this phenomenon in the history of economics, both for the logical coherence of the discipline and for its societal relevance, occurred in the publication in 1936 of John Maynard Keynes's *General Theory of Employment, Interest, and Money*.[19]

The important fact we have noticed, the scientific fact that hypotheses can be disproved but cannot be proved, rests, it will be clear, on the concomitant postulate of the ultimacy of the laws of chance. This postulate, it is worthy of note, affects the issue in two ways. First, even if it should be the case that in a given situation or as a result of a given scientific experiment the facts should confirm the hypothesis, the assumption of the laws of chance nevertheless implies that somewhere, at some time, a fact or a constellation of facts might conceivably be found to exist which disproves and dislodges the hypothesis. Many scientific hypotheses have no doubt had a long life and an ultimate demise. Second, the very testing procedure of scientific hypotheses itself invokes the law of chance. It recognizes that given the assumed randomness of every scientific universe of inquiry, it cannot be expected that observable facts will ever fit the hypothesis exactly and with complete precision. It is for this reason that we were careful to refer in the foregoing to the question of whether the facts "accorded sufficiently closely" with the hypothesis to grant it, in the case in hand, provisional confirmation. It is to establish acceptable criteria of "sufficiently closely" that the laws of statistical probability are invoked and questions of the following kind are asked: Do the facts reside sufficiently close to that conjuncture that could be predicted by the hypothesis, such that their understandable, and in a probabilistic sense predictable, deviation from the hypothesis can be assumed to be due solely to the operation of chance? Or do the facts reside sufficiently far from the implication of the hypothesis, outside the so-called limits of statistical significance, to warrant the conclusion that the deviation cannot be ascribed solely to chance and that therefore the hypothesis under test must be rejected?

The foregoing, conceivably, may appear an excessively long digression into scientific methodology. But its purpose is served by noticing that in the very nature of the case, in the very fabric of contemporary thought, we are here brought face to face with the modern dialecticism. This is what we have referred to as the rationalist-irrationalist dialecticism in which modern man swings between the assumption that he can know everything and the realization that in a final sense he knows nothing. It is this dialecticism, moreover, that provides a direct linkage between the methodological preoccupation of economics, at least in the hands of empirical practitioners if not completely in the debates of the methodologists, and the contemporary intellectual culture.

In other words, we can now crystallize the current status of economics in relation to the thought systems we have discussed by noting two important characteristics: first, the linkage of empirical methodology we have just observed; and second, the fact that at the present time, as throughout its history, economics is grounded in what we have referred to as immanentistic philosophic presuppositions. Without making any attempt to be exhaustive in such a classification, the subject partook heavily of psychologism in its nineteenth-century dependence on the notions of the "utility-maximizing" hedonistic calculus; it involved a historicism and materialism in its socialistic dissent from the earlier classical tradition that has been revived in the contemporary recrudescence of Marxian thought; and in its more ingenious theoretical forms it has succumbed at the present time to a rather thoroughgoing mathematicism. This latter has followed from the highly articulate concern with axiomatic formulations of economic theory and from, one has reason to fear, a widespread capitulation to a logicism that is in danger of taking the subject away from a very immediate real world and empirical relevance. At the same time, there is every evidence that the economists' escape into mathematicism is related to the pressures for epistemological security in the face of the disarrangement and disorder in the world, which, it becomes clear on reflection, is in turn an expression of the failure of the economic world to exhibit the niceties and the solaces of automatic harmonies.

* * *

We shall comment more fully in the following chapter on some of the points that have just been made. It will be convenient to do so by way of noting some aspects of the historical development of the subject, particularly as that throws light on the economists' own articulated concern for the larger philosophic and cultural issues we have raised. Immediately, however, it will be useful to conclude this brief delineation of our intellectual and cultural condition with some minimal observations on a final aspect of the relation between contemporary thought movements and Christian perspectives.

As philosophy has moved more deeply into logic and language and away from metaphysics, the contact between philosophy and theology, at least at the professional level, has shifted. Philosophy has become concerned not so much with the viability, or competitive ability, of alternative systems of belief, or even with the adequacy or structural coherence of competitive presuppositions that underlie systems of belief, but with the issue of the meaningfulness of religious and theological statements and questions. Logical analysis, at the level of professional philosophy, is directed to the investigation of how the words and sentence constructions used in theology are related to ordinary usages.

The publication of Professor A. J. Ayer's *Language, Truth, and Logic* in 1936, with its statement of logical positivism, has been followed by still further and massive shifting of ground. The details are rehearsed to an extent, in fact, in Ayer's introductory essay in the 1946 reissue of his book,[20] and valuable discussion occurs also in the first two contributions to the Antony G. Flew and Alasdair MacIntyre volume on *New Essays in Philosophical Theology,* in the important symposium *The Revolution in Philosophy,*[21] which Gilbert Ryle edited from a series of talks on the British Broadcasting Corporation's Third Programme, and in J. O. Urmson's *Philosophical Analysis.*[22] For our present purposes, even though significant and interpretatively meaningful lags have occurred between the shifts in thought fashions and empirical habits and orientations, one of the main advances was the realization that the meaningfulness of statements could not properly be adjudicated only and exclusively by empirical verification. Thus, for example, statements of what is regarded by an individual as right or wrong are conceivably recognizable as emotive statements that are not open to verification by empirical methods. But they should nevertheless, surely, be regarded as having meaning, or as saying something meaningful. Or take the question whether statements about God, for example a statement regarding the compatibility of the goodness of God with what appears empirically to contradict that goodness, can function as meaningful statements in the absence of any conceivable means of testing their truth. Perhaps in this case a possible future occurrence, for example the prediction of it as part of the Christian's eschatological hope, may be taken by the analyst to meet the criteria of meaning.

The claim usually advanced by the logical positivists was that because language about God and other traditional theological categories could not be empirically verified it was meaningless, or, at best, meant something quite different from that of ordinary usage. Conceivably, also, it could mean something different from what the speaker himself intended. The point to grasp, therefore, is that this position itself represented a considerable shift from earlier forms of atheism. For whereas atheism might argue that the statements of Christian theology on numbers of questions were false, the logical positivists argued that the statements were not so much false as meaningless. This was the case because the questions to which they were addressed were not themselves real questions at all. But, as we have said, this hard, empirically positivistic stance has softened. And, indeed, there are signs that philosophers themselves are to an extent disenchanted with the almost exclusive domination of philosophy by the subsequent vogue of language analysis. As Colin Brown has pointed out, the recent symposium edited by H. D. Lewis, *Clarity Is Not Enough: Essays in Criticism of Linguistic Philosophy,*[23] instances the new awareness, and the same author's *Philosophy of Religion*[24] also contains a valuable discussion.

Attention might be drawn also to a relevant and interesting observation of A. J. Ayer in his *Language, Truth, and Logic.* He draws a distinction between what he calls the "strong" and the "weak" sense of the term "verification" and says, "A proposition is said to be verifiable, in the strong sense, if, and only if, its truth could be conclusively established in experience. But it is verifiable, in the weak sense, if it is possible for experience to render it probable."[25] This importation to the discussion of an admissible probability criterion provides a linkage with the probability theorizing about which we have spoken earlier in this chapter and which can be seen coming to the fore both in forms of modern theologizing and in widening applications of the scientific method.

But what, finally, is the Christian's response to the problems raised and to the attacks upon his position of faith from the direction of analytical philosophy? Two things can be said. First, the experiential character of the Christian religion implies that it is in fact possible to know the truth of what it declares on the basis of the self-attestation of Christ's word in the self-attesting Scriptures. The Christian religion is, on its deepest experiential, or its genuinely existential level, an "I know" religion. It is not a probabilistic religion at all. Second, the basis of Christian knowledge and of the certainties of the faith as mediated by the Holy Spirit via their perspicuous inscripturation turns finally upon the meaning of the fact of Christian regeneration. We have referred to that already in terms of Kuyper's argument for "palingenesis" in relation to the possibility and validity of science. We shall not examine its further implications for Christian belief at this point.

But here we have, in the summary observations we have made in this and the preceding section, some firmer indications of the points of confluence of the levels of contemporary thought we have taken as our principal concern. We turn immediately to the emergence of a number of these categories of thought in the development of the economics discipline.

4

The Economists' Perspective

Two aspects of the history of thought bear on the perspectives we are in course of establishing. We shall discuss them briefly and in a rather highly selective fashion in this chapter. First, what were the ways in which some of the important questions in economic analysis actually came to expression historically, noting in particular the questions of economic self-interest and economic harmonies which largely determined the scope and preoccupation of the mainstream of the science into the twentieth century? And, second, what have been the attitudes of some of the principal architects of economic science to the questions of critique we are now concerned with? How, for example, have the distinguished economists of the past regarded the contact of their subject with Christian thought and Christian categories? We have observed that they were not all silent on these matters, and it will provide an important perspective to bring their contributions and discussions on relevant points into better focus. In doing so, within the selective and abbreviated scope permitted in this connection, it will be useful to note also some of the more important and relevant comments by other interpreters of social and economic thought. Progress will best be made by allowing the discussion on these questions to interweave to some extent and throw light upon each other as we proceed.

It is, as is widely known, in Adam Smith's *Inquiry into the*

Nature and the Causes of the Wealth of Nations, first published in 1776, that the beginning of systematic English economics is usually discovered. There had appeared in England during the late seventeenth and throughout the eighteenth century a large body of writing, much of it in pamphlet and occasional form, that it would be unwise to dismiss completely as "preanalytic" or "prescientific," to adapt a phrase from Joseph Schumpeter.[1] John Locke, George Berkeley, David Hume, John Law, and others, notably Richard Cantillon and Sir James Steuart, had all made significant contributions to the consolidation of an analytical, scientific tradition in English economic thought.[2]

But Smith's influential *Wealth of Nations* introduced in a new form the notion of the pervasive importance and the pervasively beneficial effects of the consistent pursuit of individual personal self-interest. Smith argued, for example, "It is not from the benevolence of the butcher, the brewer, or the baker, that we expect our dinner, but from their regard to their own interest. We address ourselves, not to their humanity but to their self-love, and never talk to them of our own necessities but of their advantage."[3] At this point, there entered into the mainstream of thought the crystallized and positively articulated doctrine of what became known as the "invisible hand" in economic affairs. This was in essence the doctrine that the consistent pursuit of individual economic self-interest would lead automatically, via the interdependent market mechanism in the system, to the maximum benefit for society as a whole.

In one of its forms this doctrine implied that the "invisible hand" of unfettered economic activities would automatically guide the economy to a situation of full employment, thus leaving no residue of unemployed workers in the nation and conducing again to the maximum benefit of all. Of course, the facts belied the theory. And economic theory gained a new level of empirical relevance only when John Maynard Keynes and others in the twentieth century had resurrected to respectability some of the eighteenth-century notions that had argued to the contrary.

The invisible hand doctrine will be relevant to the attitudes that should be taken, from the perspective of a Christian inter-

The Economists' Perspective

pretation, to the problems of employment and aggregative economic welfare. Smith's doctrine established and substantially consolidated into English economic thought the cognate politico-economic doctrine of laissez-faire. It meant, in one of its aspects, that the economic system functioned with the greatest efficiency and benefit when the participation of the state and the government in economic affairs was kept to a minimum.

If, however, Smith's influential doctrine of the invisible hand could actually be shown to be operative, the rejoinder would thereby have been given to the frequent plea of earlier decades, the plea summarized, for example, in Sir Josiah Child's *Discourse about Trade* (1690): "It is our duty to God and nature so to provide for and employ the poor."[4] It is as though we hear again the cry of Isaiah the prophet: "What mean ye that ye . . . grind the faces of the poor?" (Isa. 3:15). Or in the stark language of the Proverbs (10:15), from the text that appeared on the title page of Jacob Vanderlint's *Money Answers All Things* in 1734: "The destruction of the poor is their poverty."[5]

This important nexus of issues, the status of the poor, the healthy functioning or otherwise of the economic system, the problems of depression and hunger and unemployment that torture and humiliate, along with the agony of inflation that robs all men of their rightful property and wealth—these questions must exercise the minds of Christian thinkers as they consider the rightness and wrongness of economic institutions and policies. But the Smithian tradition of laissez-faire could not be expected, from a Christian perspective, to produce the generalized beneficial results that might be hoped for from it. Considerations of greed, rapacity, selfishness, monopoly, and exploitation, as indeed the sheer difficulties of adjustment of complex economic mechanisms, might be expected to keep on getting in the way. Indeed, Smith himself had doubts about the amenability and the rectitude and tractability of human nature adequate to ensure the smooth realization of laissez-faire benefits. And a significant body of literature could be cited to indicate the extent to which, in the early nineteenth-century period of classical economics, significant economic functions of the state were in fact envisaged. A pure and untrammeled state of economic laissez-faire has never existed or been able to exist.[6]

But Smith's bequest of laissez-faire and the invisible hand doctrine was nonetheless real.

> The annual revenue of every society is always precisely equal to the exchangeable value of the annual produce of its industry, or rather is precisely the same thing with that exchangeable value. As every individual, therefore, endeavors as much as he can both to employ his capital in the support of domestic industry, and so to direct that industry that its produce may be of the greatest value; every individual necessarily labors to render the annual revenue of the society as great as he can. He generally, indeed, neither intends to promote the public interest, nor knows how much he is promoting it. By preferring the support of domestic to that of foreign industry, he intends only his own security; and by directing that industry in such a manner as its produce may be of the greatest value, he intends only his own gain, and he is in this, as in many other cases, *led by an invisible hand* to promote an end which was no part of his intention.[7]

These classical economic notions, the invisible hand and the guarantee of automatic full utilization of the nation's resources, quickly solidified into a firm orthodoxy. There was, as we have said, a substream of dissent, and Jeremy Bentham, for example, writing at much the same time, objected to precisely these two points of classical dogma. Elie Halévy, in his *The Growth of Philosophic Radicalism*,[8] points out that for both Bentham and Smith "the object of society is the identity of interests." For Bentham, "the identity of interests is not realized spontaneously: therefore in order to establish it the law must intervene." For Smith, on the other hand, "the identity of interests is realized spontaneously: therefore, if it is to be realized, it is necessary for the law not to intervene." Similarly, Terence Hutchison has written in his insightful "Bentham as an Economist" of "Bentham's . . . scepticism as to the methodology of equilibrium theorizing and the economic harmonies."[9] Unfortunately, as Hutchison observes, Bentham's "writings on monetary theory found no disciples to follow them up."[10]

The Economists' Perspective

It thus became a part of the classical orthodoxy to argue for the validity of what became known as "the impossibility of general overproduction." To argue that there could not be a general overproduction of commodities in the economic system was to argue that there could not be a redundancy of goods produced, because there could not exist a general deficiency of demand for goods. There could not therefore exist a general deficiency of demand for labor to produce such goods, and there could not be a situation of generalized unemployment. The remarkable feature of the history of economic thought is that this theorem continued to attract allegiance throughout the postclassical period, through David Ricardo, James Mill, and others, with a dissent from Malthus that failed again to break the crust of orthodoxy, and with a general subscription in spite of some equivocation from John Stuart Mill in the middle of the nineteenth century. On past the neoclassicists, who from 1870 onward became primarily concerned with other aspects of the discipline, the doctrine continued right up to the fourth decade of the twentieth century. It was then that Keynes's alternative theoretical system exposed the fallacies of the classical school. It was a pity that for a hundred and fifty years economic analysis had been shunted onto a wrong and empirically irrelevant track, and not until economists were stared in the face by the situation in the United States, for example, where some 25 percent of the work force was unemployed, could the reality of fact at last overpower the fallacy of irrelevant theory.

The theorem that there could not be a general overproduction or a general deficiency of monetary demand for goods rested on the transparently fallacious proposition that the money values, or the money incomes, earned from producing goods would automatically be spent by the income earners on purchasing goods. The argument was logically tidy, except, unfortunately, for the realism of its premises. The possibility of generalized unemployment was precluded by the assumptions that money income would all be spent, that the money supply in the economy would continue to circulate at the same rate, and that a smoothly functioning general equilibrium at the full employment level of the nation's resources would therefore continue to exist.

But the fallacy, of course, should have been clearly seen. John Locke, in fact, writing in the last decade of the seventeenth century, had made the point clear. "The money of the nation," he said, "may lie dead, and thereby prejudice trade."[11] The classical theorem argued, on the other hand, that changes may occur in the *composition* of the total demand for goods, meaning that changes may occur in the commodity structure of trade and production. There may thereby be temporary unemployment in particular lines of activity. But this, it was claimed, would be only a matter of temporary frictional adjustment, and again the maintenance of the overall level of employment would be guaranteed by the fact that in one way or another the total money incomes would continue to be spent. There would therefore be no seriously dislocating interruptions to the smoothly circulating flow of money through the system. John Locke was, from the classical point of view, simply wrong when he feared that money may "lie dead."

But, of course, John Locke may very well be right, as Keynes was finally able to convince his professional colleagues in 1936, and a general depression in the economy might well occur. On the other hand, conditions of excess monetary expenditure may develop, or conditions may emerge in which producers reduce their willingness or ability to supply commodities at previously existing prices, or conditions in which the suppliers of labor are no longer willing to supply their services at previously existing wage rates—all pointing to possible inflationary disequilibrium in the economy. We shall note some aspects of these possible developments in a later chapter.

* * *

A number of cognate questions were canvassed as the economics literature developed from the pamphlet to the treatise stage. Some attention was given, for example, to the economics, as to the morality, of luxury expenditure. David Hume in the

The Economists' Perspective

middle of the eighteenth century distinguished between what he referred to as "innocent luxury" and "vicious luxury." He argued that the encouragement of consumers' demand by the former would be a stimulus to economic development and prosperity. In particular, in this demand he saw a key to the development of new manufactures, new wants, and new satisfactions.[12]

The notion that the expenditure of the rich provided employment opportunities for the poor was widely discussed in the eighteenth century before the appearance of Adam Smith's *Wealth of Nations*. Berkeley's *Querist* and Bernard de Mandeville's *Fable of the Bees* have become well known in this connection. In the *Querist,* published in three parts in 1735-37, Berkeley raised many well-directed questions on the nature and healthy viability of a monetary economic system. He asks, for example, "Whether the industry of the lower part of our people doth not much depend on the expense of the upper?"[13] Similarly, "Whether building would not peculiarly encourage all other arts in this kingdom?" and "whether smiths, masons, bricklayers, plaisterers, carpenters, joyners, tylers, plummers, glaziers would not all find employment if the humour of building prevailed?" And again, "Whether he who employs men in buildings *and manufactures* doth not put life in the country, and whether the neighborhood round him be not observed to thrive?" Such arguments as these could be multiplied at length to illustrate Berkeley's proposition that the circulation of money and the stimulation of monetary demand "promoted" industry and exerted magnified effects on the level of economic activity at large.[14]

The luxury question was also canvassed in Mandeville's satirical poem.[15] Joan Robinson interprets the work as satirizing "the conflict between piety and economics"[16] and points out that when the bees were one day "smitten with virtue and began to lead a sober life, eschewing pomp and pride, and adopting frugal, modest ways," a "dreadful slump" ensued. Mandeville had observed, probably by way of an attempt to expose the multiple standards of a supposedly Christian society: "Luxury employed a million of the poor, and odious pride a million more."[17] Dr. Samuel Johnson appears to have understood and agreed with

Mandeville's economics: "You cannot spend money in luxury without doing good to the poor. Nay, you do more good to them by spending it in luxury than by giving it; for by spending it in luxury you make them exert industry, whereas by giving it you keep them idle."[18] And again, "You are much surer that you are doing good when you *pay* money to those who work, as the recompense of their labor, than when you *give* money merely in charity."[19]

But the concept of the beneficial effects of such expenditures, particularly in the form in which Mandeville had stated it, was not without its critics. George Blewitt, for example, acknowledged that "the grand maxim on which this treatise [Mandeville's] of luxury is founded is, that consumption breeds riches." But, unfortunately for the cogency of his economic analysis, Blewitt continued to argue for "the absurdity of supposing that frugality should enrich every single family, and impoverish a number of those families joined together in society."[20] The fallacy in the last statement was the logical fallacy that plagued much of economic reasoning for the next two hundred years. It was the logical fallacy of composition, or the fallacy of imagining that what was true of a part was necessarily and for that reason true of the whole. In economics it appeared in the guise of imagining that, as it could be said that for any one family or person, considered separately and distinct from the rest of the community, saving, or what Adam Smith called parsimony, was beneficial, then it must necessarily be beneficial for every person in the economy to save. Patently, saving for one person may be beneficial for that person on the assumption that his savings could be put to work in economically profitable investment. But if everyone increased his rate of saving simultaneously, it would not necessarily be true that profitable investment opportunities would be available to absorb all of the savings being made. For savers were also both income receivers and income spenders. And to the extent that their incomes were saved rather than spent, it can be seen, they would actually be contributing to a deficiency of demand and to a tendency for the total expenditure, employment, and income streams to fall.

The Economists' Perspective

But the fallacy of composition seems always to have been a trap for economic analysis. Josiah Tucker, in the late preclassical period, anticipated the classical theorem regarding the impossibility of general overproduction in his negative answer to the question, "Whether it is possible in the nature of things for all trades and professions to be overstocked?"[21] He had asked in reply, "If a particular trade is at any time overstocked, will not the disease cure itself?" And he gave an answer that was the more usual province of the next century of economic analysis. Consideration of frictional unprofitability would adjust the use of resources to demands in particular markets, and there was no reason why factors of production in general, workers or machinery, need remain permanently unemployed. The same point was made a little later by Francis Hutcheson, a mentor of Adam Smith, in reply to Mandeville. Money not spent in one way would be spent in another.[22] This theory, of course, soon hardened into the firm classical orthodoxy. But we should bear in mind also the substream of dissent referred to earlier. Bentham's argument was particularly insightful. He even spoke of the problem associated with taxation revenue collections by the government, pointing out that "of the money taken by the tax . . . part would have been spent in the way of consumption,"[23] and the fall in consumption expenditures, unless offset, could be expected to lead to a reduction in prices and a lower level of employment.[24]

Bentham's arguments, however, like those of Malthus, failed to break the crust of orthodoxy, and with Ricardo's rejection of them the classical system embraced the assumption of the general validity of what became known as Say's Law.[25] This, to employ the expressive language of John Maynard Keynes, said quite simply "Supply creates its own demand."[26] In this we have the crystallization of the classical theorem discussed earlier. The "law," or postulate, said that the total incomes created in producing the national output would continue to be spent and respent. The production of goods created incomes, and the expenditure of those incomes would be sufficient to purchase the goods produced. The logic of this argument implied that if supply created its own demand at any given or specified level of production and employment, supply would similarly create its own demand at all conceivable levels of employment. There could not therefore exist any obstacles to the full employment of the total work force available and willing to work. It was a tidy theory, and it comfortably underpinned the notions of the laissez-faire approach to the economic world. It was a pity, however, that the facts belied the theory. It was a double pity that economic theory had to wait until the fourth decade of the twentieth century before the stubbornness of the facts forced a new theoretical conceptualization. Say's Law simply did not hold in fact. Supply did not create its own demand at all conceivable levels of employment.[27] The aggregate economic system could and did stagnate at a permanently depressed level of employment and activity.

Not all scholars, of course, have made, or agreed on the need to make, what Keynes called the "struggle of escape" from the assumptions and strictures of the classical theoretical system. But from the viewpoint of Christian desiderata, the lessons from this controversy need to be learned. First, it is necessary to avoid a false commitment to the postulates of an uninhibited laissez-faire, self-interested individualism. It is difficult to understand the characterization of the reformer John Calvin, for example, as "the father of laissez-faire capitalism."[28] Considerations of the exigencies of sin, of the characteristic structures of the fallen society to which economic analysis and policy are necessarily directed, as well as Calvin's own economic policy recommendations in Geneva, stand in the way of such a shallow characterization. Nor, on the other hand, can it be expected that economics in a Christian perspective would make a basic and determinative commitment to a collectivism or socialism in which the state or politically corporate bodies were permitted, or required, to usurp the legitimate economic functions and prerogatives of individual persons. We shall return to a further discussion of these and related questions in a later chapter.

It is of interest to notice that Thomas Chalmers, the famous Scottish theologian and preacher who held professorships in moral philosophy and economics (then referred to as political

The Economists' Perspective

economy) at St. Andrews and in theology at Edinburgh, published an important treatise *On Political Economy* in 1832.[29] In this work Chalmers stands clearly with the Malthusians and a small group of scholars, including Sismondi and, at a slightly earlier date, Lauderdale, at the head of a campaign against what we have referred to as Say's Law.[30] Chalmers, in other words, found it impossible to accept an economics built on the classical postulates of automatic full employment and maximum social welfare. The positions taken by Chalmers and Malthus against the classical economics were precisely those taken more than a century later, with more systematic completeness and logical consistency, by Keynes. Keynes explicitly acknowledged Chalmers's anticipation of his own achievement, and he expressed regret that the "answer which Ricardo gave to the contentions of Malthus and Chalmers seems to have been accepted as sufficient by most later economists."[31] Chalmers, a Reformed theologian whom John Macleod has referred to as "far the most celebrated" of "the group of divines who adorned the early years of the Victorian age,"[32] reveals in his *Political Economy* a deep concern for socioeconomic conditions and for the state of the people at that time. It was for this reason, against the perspective of the insights his biblical theology gave him, that this Reformed theologian and economist found it necessary to turn aside in his economics from the barren classical assumptions.

Joan Robinson, in her *Economic Philosophy*, has made an interesting judgment in concluding that "Keynes brought back the moral problem that *laissez-faire* had abolished."[33] The latter, we recall, flowering from the Smithian postulate regarding the social beneficence of consistent individual action from the motive of self-interest, had generated an ideology that was supported by the preoccupation of economics with the notion of equilibrium. This was the condition to which the economic system would automatically return, it was thought, if it were for any reason dislodged from it. As to practical affairs, Joan Robinson observes, "the policy recommended was *laissez-faire,* and there was no need to describe in any detail how to do nothing."[34] Though her conclusion is no doubt too all-embracing and is open to considerable qualification on a close reading of the nineteenth- and early twentieth-century texts, the point of the comment is apposite. Recalling the argument of Mandeville that "private vices," in particular luxury expenditure, may be "public benefits" by affording employment to otherwise idle workers, Robinson concludes as follows on Keynes's *General Theory:* "What made the *General Theory* so hard to accept was not its intellectual content, which in a calm mood can easily be mastered, but its shocking implications. Worse than private vices being public benefits, it seemed that the new doctrine was the still more disconcerting proposition that private virtues (of thriftiness and careful husbandry) were public vices."[35] But, Robinson continues, "we have seen our way through this now," and the *General Theory* has made it "impossible to believe any longer in an automatic reconciliation of conflicting interests into a harmonious whole."[36]

It would be a thoroughgoing mistake, of course, to imagine that Keynes's own work was informed by a confessedly Christian perspective. Quite to the contrary, as we shall see in brief comments at a later point in this chapter on the philosophical predilections of certain famous economists. We cannot, therefore, commit ourselves to all that Keynes said on either economic thought or economic policy simply because we have found him reaching for a demonstrably significant analytical proposition. But it is of interest to notice, on a point of basic economic philosophy, the position Keynes took in 1926, some ten years before the *General Theory* was published. In the first paragraph of his essay, "The End of Laissez-Faire," he wrote:

> Let us clear from the ground the metaphysical or general principles upon which, from time to time, *laissez-faire* has been founded. It is *not* true that individuals possess a prescriptive "natural liberty" in their economic activities. There is no "compact" conferring perpetual rights on those who Have or on those who Acquire. The world is *not* so governed from above that private and social interests always coincide. It is *not* so managed here below that in practice they coincide. It is *not* a correct deduction from the Principles of Economics that enlightened self-interest always operates in the public interest. Nor is it true that self-interest generally *is* enlight-

ened: more often individuals acting separately to promote their own ends are too ignorant or too weak to attain even these. Experience does *not* show that individuals, when they make up a social unit, are always less clear-sighted than when they act separately.[37]

In his economic-social philosophy Keynes is here harking back to the important body of eighteenth-century thought which, we have already observed, was unfortunately submerged by the classical economics that served the newly emerging industrial interests so well. Sir James Steuart, whose *Principles of Political Economy* in 1767 was largely concerned with what he saw as the natural tendencies in the economic system to disequilibrium and depression, nevertheless recognized the importance of the freedom of individual economic action. But he did not stay, as did his successors, with the assumption of an identity between the "self-interest" of individuals and of the nation as a whole. His objectives and methods were quite different from those of the utilitarian economics of the century that followed. Given the basic objective of the full employment of the people, Steuart had no confidence that the conjunction of economic forces would always be such, if left to themselves, as to achieve this end. He had no faith in the "invisible hand" of the classicists and in the natural harmony of interests this presupposed. If left to itself, a position of economic equilibrium, or "the balance of work and demand," will be destroyed, and a considerable section of Book II of the *Principles* is devoted to the explanation of why this should be so.[38]

Steuart recalled John Locke's perceptive point that "the money of the nation may lie dead and thereby prejudice trade" in his argument, "When money does not circulate, it is the same things as if it did not exist."[39] He commented also on the luxury controversy of the eighteenth century by referring explicitly to the deleterious effects of hoarding money and of interruptions to the circular flow of money expenditures: "In proportion as the consumers become extravagant, the producers become wealthy. . . . As the former become frugal and economical, the latter languish; when those begin to hoard, and to adopt a simple life, these are extinguished."[40] Given the likelihood of damaging interruptions to trade activity and economic health if reliance were placed only on uncoordinated individual behavior, Steuart saw it consistently as an area of responsibility of the "statesman" (a phrase he used throughout his work to refer to the government authorities) "to provide . . . employment for all his people."[41] "The nation's wealth must be kept entire, *and made to circulate,* so as to provide subsistence and employment for everybody."[42] "It is, therefore, the business of a statesman, who intends to promote circulation, to be upon his guard against every cause of stagnation; and when he has it not in his power to remove these political obstructions, as I may call them, by drawing the coin of the country out of its repositories, he ought . . . to facilitate the introduction of symbolic money to supply its place."[43]

* * *

Edwin Seligman, the distinguished occupant of the McVickar professorship of political economy in Columbia University some fifty years ago, after observing "that the history of mankind is the history of man in society, and therefore social history in its broadest sense," goes on to argue: "The question has arisen as to the fundamental causes of this social development—the reason of these great changes in human thought and human life which form the conditions of progress. No more profound and far-reaching question can occupy our attention; for upon the correct answer depends our whole attitude toward life itself."[44] We are not at this time primarily concerned with the structure or validity of Seligman's analysis or even with the detailed form of the "historical materialism" thesis he discussed. We shall reserve for the moment a comment on the materialist or the socialist and Marxist dissent of the nineteenth century. Our interest here, rather, is the important methodological question opened to us by this classic argument.

The enigma of man is as old as the history it embellishes and as new as the successive generations it puzzles. "What is man?" we hear the Psalmist ask,[45] and we know with an instinct that will not be erased that man and his culture are finally explicable

The Economists' Perspective

only from vantage points that larger categories provide. Perhaps we remember paradise. Perhaps the embers of memory persuade us we once knew a nobler estate. The Oxford economist D. L. Munby is no doubt correct in deciding that the ills and the jarring disharmonies of our culture are "the price of original sin."[46] But certainly the social and economic problem is not amenable to full explanation from a single-valued and immanentistic perspective.[47] Seligman acknowledged that the economic category established by the thesis he examined failed of itself to provide significant explanatory results. "From the purely philosophical standpoint," he concluded, "it may be confessed that the theory, especially in its extreme form, is no longer tenable as the universal explanation of all human life. No monistic interpretation of humanity is possible. . . . As a philosophical doctrine of universal validity, the theory of 'historical materialism' can no longer be successfully defended."[48]

To say, as we have done, that an adequate approach to cultural and economic inquiry cannot be built on a single-valued perspective is to echo a contention that has frequently occupied serious minds in their analysis of the social question. T. S. Eliot, the British poet, essayist, and culturist, addressed the same point in his work *The Idea of a Christian Society,* in which he was "concerned with . . . the organization of values, and a direction of religious thought which must inevitably proceed to a criticism of political and economic systems."[49] He quotes with approval the proposition that "men have lived by *spiritual* institutions (of some kind) in every society, and also by *political* institutions, and indubitably, by *economic* activities. Admittedly, they have, at different periods, tended to put their trust mainly in one of the three as the real cement of society, but at no time have they wholly excluded the others, because it is impossible to do so."[50] The critical question, of course, relates to the nature of the coordinating rubric under which one's categories of social evaluation are themselves brought into harmony and to a mutual interdependence. We can agree with the prominent American economist Kenneth Boulding, for example, that in the matter of the ethico-economic interrelationship, "at the policy level economics without ethics is a lever without a fulcrum."[51] But we can hardly share his despair and agnosticism when he concludes, in his response to the problem of what determines "the dominant value system" in society, that "this is a question to which at the present time there seems to be no good answers."[52]

Eliot again has pointed his criticism in a relevant direction in his comment that "the more highly industrialized the country, the more easily a materialistic philosophy will flourish in it, and the more deadly the philosophy will be. . . . The tendency of unlimited industrialism is to create bodies of men and women—of all classes—detached from tradition, alienated from religion, and susceptible to mass suggestion: in other words, a mob. And a mob will be no less a mob if it is well fed, well clothed, well housed, and well disciplined."[53] Eliot quotes with approval J. H. Oldham's comment:

> "May our salvation lie in an attempt to recover our Christian heritage, not in the sense of going back to the past, but of discovering in the central affirmations and insights of the Christian faith new spiritual energies to regenerate and vitalise our sick society? Does not the public repudiation of the whole Christian scheme of life in a large part of what was once known as Christendom force to the front the question whether the path of wisdom is not rather to attempt to work out a Christian doctrine of modern society and to order our national life in accordance with it."[54]

Of course, there are obstacles in the way of such an achievement. Eliot acknowledges that a "common failure lies in putting the human response first, and so thinking of Christianity as primarily a *religion*. Consequently there is among us a tendency to view the problems of the day in the light of what is practically possible, rather than in the light of what is imposed by the principles of that truth to which the Church is set to bear witness."[55] In other words, Eliot, whose analysis itself falls short of a consistently Christian argument, concludes,

> To justify Christianity because it provides a foundation of morality, instead of showing the necessity of Christian mo-

The Economists' Perspective

rality from the truth of Christianity, is a very dangerous inversion; and we may reflect, that a good deal of the attention of totalitarian states has been devoted, with a steadiness of purpose not always found in democracies, to providing their national life with a foundation of morality—the wrong kind perhaps, but a good deal more of it. It is not enthusiasm, but dogma, that differentiates a Christian from a pagan society.[56]

Similarly, Munby has reminded us of Pusey's observation a century ago, "All things must speak of God, refer to God, or they are atheistic. History, without God, is a chaos without design, or end, or aim. Political economy, without God, would be a selfish teaching about the acquisition of wealth, making the larger portion of mankind animate machines for its production."[57] And he quotes from F. D. Maurice to comparable effect: "I fear all economics, politics, physics, are in danger of becoming Atheistic: not when they are worst, but even when they are best; that Mill, Fourier, Humboldt, are more in danger of making a system which shall absolutely exclude God, and suffice without Him, than any less faithful and consistent thinkers."[58]

Perhaps, however, in this initial look at the breadth or otherwise of the categories of socioeconomic inquiry, it will be of most interest to those familiar with the history of economic thought to refer again to Adam Smith. We are indebted to James Bonar's *Philosophy and Political Economy* for preserving a significant but little known section of the first edition of Smith's *Theory of Moral Sentiments*. Smith had published this work a couple of decades before his more famous and widely known *Wealth of Nations,* and a good deal of controversy has ensued regarding the possible grounds on which his seemingly alternating positions in the two separate works should be harmonized. It is to the *Moral Sentiments* that we can look for a closer view of the ethics behind Smith's economic position, though the connection with the *Wealth of Nations* is tenuous. The following comment, moreover, was omitted from all editions of the *Moral Sentiments* subsequent to the first, and Smith has therefore left a significant line of thought unfortunately undeveloped. The comment is recalled as a counterpoint to what, on the basis of the mainstream of Smith's work and his principal bequest to economics, might be regarded as his optimistic humanist and individualist philosophy.

Smith is here discussing the nature and meaning of virtue and vice, and he is examining the significance of the anthropology that underlies his analysis of human affairs:

> If we consult our natural sentiments, we are apt to fear lest before the holiness of God, vice should appear to be more worthy of punishment than the weakness and imperfection of human virtue can ever seem to be of reward. Man when about to appear before a being of infinite perfection can feel but little confidence in his own merit or in the imperfect propriety of his own conduct. . . . If he would still hope for happiness, he is conscious that he cannot demand it from the justice, but that he must entreat it from the mercy of God. Repentance, sorrow, humiliation, contrition at the thought of his past conduct, are, upon this account, the sentiments which become him, and seem to be the only means which he has left for appeasing that wrath which, he knows, he has justly provoked. . . . Some other intercession, some other sacrifice, some other atonement, he imagines, must be made for him beyond what he himself is capable of making before the purity of the Divine justice can be reconciled to his manifold offences.[59]

But this, of course, is not the Smith that has come down through the history of thought, nor the Smith with which economics has substantial familiarity.

* * *

We have spoken of a tension that raises a trap for Christian economic thought. Questions, we have seen, of capitalism, socialism, individualism, and collectivism, are amenable to their fullest understanding only in the light of deeper issues. At this point, the rights of the individual and of individual dignity and freedom come clearly into focus. In a profound sense the great achievement of the sixteenth-century Reformation was that it released on the world the energies of the new discovery of the worth of the individual.

At the same time, a correlative principle also informs the

Christian approach to economic structures and policies. This is the principle of the avoidance of unnecessary or excessive concentrations of economic power and, in particular, the exploitation of that power. In observable instances unreasonable power and its unreasonable exercise are held by monopolistic concentrations of industry and business firms within industries. On other occasions, the illegitimate exploitation of economic power is made by trade unions for reasons of shortsighted and selfish gain. And in other instances, the undue concentration of power resides in the hands of governments or governmentally established agencies and corporations. The reasonable diffusion of power, consistent with rational criteria of social welfare and economic efficiency, is correlative to the economic and the welfare connotation of the dignity and freedom of the individual.

Perspective on these tensions can be established by noting the ambivalence on these very points within the English classical school. Adam Smith, we have seen, bequeathed to classical orthodoxy the notions of beneficent individualism—laissez-faire—and the "invisible hand" that guaranteed the aggregative harmony of economic interests in society. Smith also had doubts about the robustness of human nature adequate to support, on the level of morality and ethics, the automaticity and beneficence of the equilibrium which, on the other side of his argument, his economics envisaged. In fact, it is hardly correct to suggest, as Seligman has done, that "the first isolated mutterings of discontent came from France. Simonde de Sismondi already, in 1819, accused the orthodox school of 'forgetting the men for the things; of sacrificing the end to the means; of producing a beautiful logic, but a total forgetfulness of man and human nature."[60] For Smith himself has given us some worried and enlightened passages on the state of man and human nature.

Jacob Viner, for example, concluded in a classic essay that "Adam Smith was not a doctrinaire advocate of *laissez-faire*. He saw a wide and elastic range of activity for government, and he was prepared to extend it even further. . . . Smith saw that self-interest and competition were sometimes treacherous to the public interest they were supposed to serve, and he was prepared to have government exercise some measure of control over them where the need could be shown and the competence of government for the task demonstrated."[61] The question was one of bringing into existence the appropriate framework of law and regulatory institutions within which the independent actions of economic entities could be channeled toward the general good.[62] Lionel Robbins, in a masterly treatment of English classical economic thought, has observed that the issue was simply that

> so far from the system of economic freedom being something which will certainly come into being if things are just left to their course, it can only come into being if they are *not* left to take their course, if a conscious effort is made to create the highly artificial environment which is necessary if it is to function properly. The invisible hand which guides men to promote ends which were no part of their intention, is not the hand of some god or some natural agency independent of human effort; it is the hand of the lawgiver, the hand which withdraws from the sphere of the pursuit of self-interest those possibilities which do not harmonize with the public good. There is absolutely no suggestion that the market can furnish everything; on the contrary, it can only begin to furnish anything when a whole host of other things have been furnished in another way.[63]

Smith speaks repeatedly of the "uniform, constant, and uninterrupted effort of every man to better his condition,"[64] and he frequently rests his case for the mobility of labor and resources on such an assumption. But his view of human nature and its proclivities, outside, that is, of the institutional framework of law and justice necessary to contain it, is in some respects pessimistic: "Such, it seems, is the natural insolence of man, that he almost always disdains to use the good instrument, except when he cannot or dare not use the bad one."[65] And in an eloquent passage that concludes Book I of the *Wealth of Nations,* Smith points out the natural conflicts of interest that can arise between the public on the one hand and the merchant and manufacturing classes on the other. The latter, Smith says, are "an order of men, whose interest is never exactly the same with that of the

The Economists' Perspective

public, who have generally an interest to deceive and even to oppress the public, and who accordingly have, upon many occasions, both deceived and oppressed it."[66]

A significant instance of Smith's concern for adequate institutional arrangements occurs in an argument bearing on monetary and banking regulations. The point had to do with prohibitions against the excessive issue of small denomination notes. "Such regulations," Smith acknowledged, designed in the interests of financial stability and "to restrain private people . . . may, no doubt, be considered . . . a violation of natural liberty." But by analogy, "the obligation of building party walls, in order to prevent the communication of fire, is a violation of natural liberty, exactly of the same kind with the regulations of the banking trade which are here proposed."[67]

It is unnecessary to multiply further the instances of tension and ambivalence, and the shifting philosophic foundations of classical thought, to expose the significance of the fact that, as H. F. R. Catherwood has put it succinctly, "the idea of a golden age of complete *laissez-faire* is almost certainly a myth."[68] Finally, there is the evaluative argument of Jacob Viner in a recent essay: "Smith maintained (in the *Theory of Moral Sentiments*) that man is endowed by God with his moral sentiments and that these sentiments bind men to each other *because the deity so made them in its concern for the happiness of mankind.* . . . Here Smith was, of course, invoking 'final causes' or 'the invisible hand.' "[69] The question at issue is the extent to which Smith did or did not subscribe to what has been called the "optimistic deism" of his time and what his view of human nature was as a result. Viner, in the argument just referred to, is focusing our attention on the notion of happiness, not only as a social and economic motivation of individuals' action, but, more significantly, as the imagined objective or the end God himself had in view in His creation and government of the world. It can properly be asked whether, if Smith did "definitively commit himself to the theism of his time,"[70] as Viner supposes, he was on safe ground in doing so. For it can be asked whether the "harmonious order in nature guided by god"[71] operated in fact in the interests of the deity's "concern for the happiness of mankind," or, rather, in the interest of His church as the "orthodox Calvinists" who "rejected Smith's optimistic aspects" would conceivably have argued.[72] At issue is the robustness of the classical deism which, taken in conjunction with the hedonist-utilitarian foundation in economic thought, had fairly completely evacuated the earlier theism of its real and culturally determinative meaning.

* * *

This question does, however, provoke an important inquiry regarding the extent to which economists have taken conscious account of the ways or purpose of God in the world. Or perhaps the question should be whether, in the mainstream of its development, economic thought has been articulately or even implicitly conscious of either the creation activity of God, which implies man's derivative nature and responsibility to God, or God's providential preservation of the created order, which implies man's continuing dependence upon God. No significant excursion into intellectual history is necessary to establish the fact that theological thought in general, and distinctively Christian thought in particular, have only minimal contiguity with the development of the economics discipline.

For the main part, the relationship has been of the kind that William Letwin has described in *The Origins of Scientific Economics,* in an argument that strikes at the roots of economic epistemology. "There can be no doubt," Letwin concludes, "that economic theory owes its present development to the fact that some men, in thinking of economic phenomena, forcefully suspended all judgments of theology, morality, and justice, were willing to consider the economy as nothing more than an intricate mechanism, refraining for the while from asking whether the mechanism worked for good or evil."[73] Admittedly, "It was exceedingly difficult to treat economics in a scientific fashion, since every economic act, being the action of a human being, is necessarily also a moral act."[74] But that was the task, according to Letwin, that had to be accomplished in order that the subject as an academic and scientific discipline could develop. There needed to be a separation of "positive from normative knowledge,"[75] a distinction drawn "between moral and technical knowledge."[76]

Of the clear and widening breach between economics and Christian thought there can be no doubt. To pass over the earlier period of nineteenth-century development, and the heavy influence it imbibed from the atheological system of utilitarianism, Alfred Marshall, for example, the great systematizing architect of neoclassical economics, made an explicit and conscientious break with the church and its influence. Joseph Schumpeter has referred to "the process, as observed in the Cambridge [England] milieu by which Christian belief, gently and without any acerbities, was dropped by the English intelligentsia" during Marshall's lifetime (1842-1924).[77] Terence Hutchison, likewise, in his scholarly *Review of Economic Doctrines,* has referred to the achievement of academic economics at Cambridge in the last quarter of the nineteenth century as due to the fact that the architects of the system "conceived their task as belonging not in the realm of theology and metaphysics, but in clearing a site, and providing an agreed foundation for 'scientific' inquiry, and here . . . they drew no specially significant or dramatic distinction between the two broad groups of sciences included under the very rough headings of 'natural' and 'social' (or moral) sciences."[78]

The prominent economists of the nineteenth and twentieth centuries, therefore, did not establish an interdependence or even a contiguity between their intellectual discipline on the one hand, and theological or Christian thought on the other. Economics in both its individualist and collectivist expressions has deliberately set aside the possible relevance of Christian presuppositions to develop, as it imagined, a value-free and "scientific" inquiry.

In the earlier years of the nineteenth century, as the industrial revolution gathered pace and its promised benefits turned into bitter fruits for many of the working classes, the harsh conditions of industrialism raised protests against what appeared to be the harsh teachings of the political economists. The system simply did not work with the smooth beneficent efficiency which the theory posited. The classical "reconciliation of private egoism and public service," to adapt a phrase from Joan Robinson,[79] did not in fact provide the harmony of interests and the maximum generalized welfare that it promised in theory. In the significant social protest that ensued, Christians played a large part, and it is possible to see in the social history of the nineteenth century in England the ripening results of the evangelical awakening the country had experienced a hundred years previously.[80] It is not possible to examine this Christian contribution to economic affairs in detail at present, but it is not necessarily a sound historical judgment to conclude, as Munby has done, that, "as a whole the Christian witness was not impressive."[81] Munby, in fact, suggests the hypothesis that "it could be seriously argued, even taking into account the noble work of Lord Shaftesbury, that more reforms were brought into effect by the influence of Benthamism, working through people like Chadwick, the sanitary reformer, and in later years the Webbs and the Fabians, or by the aggressive militancy of the workers, than through the influences of the Churches, in a nominally Christian country."[82] But a careful look at the historical data may conclude that Shaftesbury was not as "splendidly and forlornly isolated"[83] as has been supposed.[84]

It was nevertheless true, however, that Christian practice and Christian influence were gradually confined in the nineteenth century to this level of pragmatic affairs and that the hold that Christian thought might once have enjoyed in the universities and in the scholarly professions was shaken fairly completely. This situation prevailed in economics, and the neoclassical system that developed from 1870 onward and came to maturity in the definitive edition of Marshall's *Principles* in 1920, like the Keynesian and post-Keynesian systems that followed, had virtually no formative contact with Christian thought. This development was heavily influenced on the levels of epistemology and investigative processes by the post-Kantian positivism and scientism and by the assumptions of human autonomy on which they were erected. The prominent economists of the last hundred years have generally shared the attitudes of rationalism, of one kind or another, that characterized the times, and this, to confine our comments to perhaps the most influential case, was unfortunately true of the great Alfred Marshall.

Much has been made in the history of economics of the influence on Marshall of Henry Sidgwick, the philosopher-economist of whom Marshall wrote, "I was fashioned by him. He was so to speak my spiritual father and mother."[85] On the other hand, Marshall's earlier interest in philosophy had taken him to Germany and to a study of Kant, whom he referred to as "Kant my guide, the only man I ever worshipped."[86] But Marshall, like Sidgwick before him, had reached his philosophic stance after an earlier nominal subscription to Christianity. In fact, as Munby has pointed out, in the earlier nineteenth century and even on into relatively recent times, "in the university of those days, elections to Chairs were dependent on theological rectitude rather than on any contribution to learning."[87] Munby reports an interesting situation in which in 1836 F. D. Maurice agreed to stand for election to the Chair of Political Economy at Oxford on the grounds that there appeared to be no one else ready to stand with the support of a theological party, and that "political economy is not the foundation of morals and politics, but must have them for its foundations or be worth nothing." Maurice, it is reported, knew nothing of political economy, but was prepared to "endeavor to master the details of the subject." But in the outcome, the support of the Tractarians was withdrawn from him and he did not accede to the chair.[88]

The philosophic milieu as it closed in on the economists in the formative stage of academic economics in the last half of the nineteenth century, and the effects it had on the principal scholars of the time, can probably not be more perceptively summarized than in a paragraph from Keynes's superb biographical essay on Marshall:

> Marshall's Cambridge career came just at the date which will, I think, be regarded by historians of opinion as the critical moment at which Christian dogma fell away from the serious philosophical world of England, or at any rate of Cambridge. In 1863 Henry Sidgwick, aged twenty-four, had

> subscribed to the Thirty-Nine Articles as a condition of tenure of his Fellowship, and was occupied in reading Deuteronomy in Hebrew and preparing lectures on the Acts of the Apostles. Mill, the greatest intellectual influence on the youth of the age, had written nothing which clearly indicated any divergence from received religious opinions up to his *Examination of Hamilton* in 1865. At about this time Leslie Stephen was an Anglican clergyman, James Ward a nonconformist minister, Alfred Marshall a candidate for holy orders, W. K. Clifford a High Churchman. In 1869 Sidgwick resigned his Trinity Fellowship, "to free myself from dogmatic obligations." A little later none of these could have been called Christians. Nevertheless, Marshall, like Sidgwick, was as far as possible from adopting an "anti-religious" attitude. He sympathized with Christian morals and Christian ideals and Christian incentives. There is nothing in his writings depreciating religion in any form; few of his pupils could have spoken definitively about his religious opinions. At the end of his life, he said, "Religion seems to me an attitude," and that though he had given up Theology, he believed more and more in Religion. The great change-over of the later sixties was an intellectual change, not an ethical or emotional change which belongs to a later generation, and it was a wholly intellectual debate which brought it about.[89]

It is, of course, grossly unfortunate that Keynes should here have fallen prey to a shallow misunderstanding. For we find him imagining that Marshall in particular, and economics in general, could retain a productive sense of the "Christian morals and Christian ideals and Christian incentives" when the Christian doctrine had been so definitively jettisoned. Keynes's own intellectual and professional position appears unfortunately to have been untouched by Christianity. He recorded in his memoirs the priority of the influence upon him of the philosophy of Moore. "We accepted Moore's religion," he says, "and discarded his morals. Indeed, in our opinion, one of the greatest advantages of his religion, was that it made morals unnecessary—meaning by 'religion' one's attitude towards oneself and the ultimate and by 'morals' one's attitude towards the outside world and the intermediate."[90] Keynes elaborates on his own position further in his essay, "My Early Beliefs," from which we have just quoted. Writing this

The Economists' Perspective

essay shortly before the end of his life, Keynes gives us a sad view of a great mind's failure to grasp the final truth and the true existential structure of things. We see him say that he had "no reason to shift from the fundamental intuitions of [Moore's] *Principia Ethica,* though they are much too few and too narrow to fit actual experiences"; and he acknowledges that the "pseudo-rational view of human nature" he held "led to a thinness, a superficiality, not only of judgment, but also of feeling."

A mind generously capacious and subtle, touched by the common grace that makes scientific progress and cultural achievement meaningful, Keynes nevertheless provides us with no reason to conclude that at his hands, and in the light of his revolutionary achievement, economics had made any move to the elucidation of a Christian perspective. Consolidated in the metaphysical assumptions of the autonomy of man and in the pretended epistemological sufficiency of human reason, economics has proceeded to the construction of a tidily logical, quasi-mathematical, self-contained thought system that is only now showing some signs of stirring from its self-imposed shackles of supposed ethical neutrality and the danger of worsening empirical irrelevance.

Perhaps the saddest commentary on the state of affairs in the discipline is provided by the concluding pages of the *Economic Philosophy* of Joan Robinson, whose influence at Cambridge has done perhaps more than that of any other scholar in English economics to interpret the work of Keynes. Addressing finally the moral problem, which she recognizes after all to surround economic thought and policy, Robinson can offer us only a darkened and discouraged agnosticism: "The moral problem is a conflict that can never be settled. Social life will always present mankind with a choice of evils. No metaphysical solution that can ever be formulated will seem satisfactory for long. The solutions offered by economists were no less delusory than those of the theologians that they displaced. All the same we must not abandon . . . hope."[91]

Another British economist, D. L. Munby, begins his work on *Christianity and Economic Problems* with what he sees as foundational propositions relating to "God the Creator" and "Man the Sinner."[92] It does not necessarily imply subscription to all of Munby's arguments to acknowledge the value and importance of his return to the same themes in his *God and the Rich Society*.[93] Fuller judgment will be made in due course on the adequacy or cogency of his argument that "there are no exclusively Christian answers to social problems, and no possible Christian synthesis, but that there are Christian principles and Christian standards, by which to judge the institutions and arrangements of a social and economic order, and which will guide us in action."[94] Though suspending a definitive judgment on this statement for the present, it is nevertheless clear that a great many aspects of our economic institutions and arrangements call for an evaluation from a Christian perspective. Questions of work, wealth, big business, monopolistic exploitation, trade unions, the stock exchanges, taxation systems and policies, income distribution, poverty, inflation, money, economic growth, pollution, technological advance, and the economic responsibilities of governments, all demand careful thought in the context of the Christian approach to an economically and socially complex age.

We shall comment on a number of these questions in a later chapter. It will be convenient for the present to turn to a summary consideration of the roots of economic culture, particularly as that comes into focus from a Christian perspective.

5

The Roots of Economic Culture

The economic dimension of our culture offers a vantage point from which to bring together the principal strands of our argument as it has developed to this point. The economic aspect of things is a primary contributor to what we have called our intellectual-cultural condition. There are several respects in which this is so.

First, it has been seen in the preceding chapter that as it came to maturity during the latter decades of the nineteenth century, economics deliberately set out to establish what it took to be a legitimate value-free inquiry. It became engaged, as Hutchison put it, in "clearing a site," and it conceived its task as definitively distanced from "the realms of theology and metaphysics." In this endeavor, it partook of the developing strands of individualist-humanist thought and philosophic foundations that had mounted an increasing pressure on educated opinion since the Enlightenment era. In the latter days of Victorian optimism, abetted by the capture of the social sciences by the thought forms of Darwinian evolutionary theory, economics confirmed its rootage in classical utilitarianism, substantially succumbed to the influences of methodological positivism, and thrust forward to the twentieth century the insistence that its integrity as a discipline turned on a distinctively amoral stance in the world of affairs.

The rampant individualism of the industrial revolution had encountered the socialist and collectivist dissent of the third quarter of the nineteenth century, and social legislation attests that some softening of conscience had occurred. But the dissenting voices themselves concurred with the foundational assumptions that industrial progress, technological advance, and ongoing struggles for increasing shares of what the economic machine could produce pointed to the directions in which desirable social development should occur. The economic system creaked with the stresses that advanced industrialism imposed upon it. But in the Old World the niceties and stabilities of the international gold standard still calmed the mounting rumblings of concern, and in the New World economic expansion and the rolling back of frontiers kept the drive of development alive. In both worlds, the divorce of economics and ethics was substantially, if not universally, acknowledged to be both necessary and complete. It was not until the fourth quarter of the twentieth century that theoretical advances in the discipline finally caught up with the realities and the instabilities of actual conditions, and only in recent times has a more widespread concern led to a questioning, on what appears to be fundamental as opposed to earlier peripheral dimensions, of the more comfortable complacencies.

Second, this pervasive concern to establish a value-free inquiry was both influenced by, and influenced the cultural impact and significance of, the now widespread assumptions of what earlier philosophers had posited as the autonomy of man. Here was the deposit of the Renaissance coming to full fruition. Though, as we have seen, the culturally formative notions of individualist-humanist thought were softened by the theological influences of the Reformation, nevertheless the assumption had by this time become pervasive that mankind could afford to escape, and had in fact securely escaped, from the strictures of any genuine theological concern. The poet's "I am the master of my fate" fairly completely determined attitudes to societal and cultural advance. Man's destiny was now in his own hands, and from the nineteenth to the twentieth centuries the prospects for the competence and success of social engineering seemed unarguable and assured.

Thus it emerged that when, in fact, the economic theoretical

The Roots of Economic Culture

advances of the mid-twentieth century displaced the earlier assumptions of reliable and automatic harmonies, attention turned increasingly to the possibilities of deliberately engineering the forms and structures of economic conditions. If the system was unstable, and if uncomfortable fluctuations disrupted the calmer order, then by the use of suitable economic policies, for example monetary and fiscal policies, the economic machine could be tuned to superior performance. In the earlier development of economics, theistic assumptions and any cognizance of a providential ordering of things had been rapidly displaced by a generalized deism and its logic of a definitive divine-human separation. Now there developed a conscious and consciously articulated assumption that man in society could direct his own economic and cultural evolution. If conditions were not right, it was within human competence to put them right. The twentieth century had become the century of social and economic engineering. Of course, there were voices of dissent that will be noted in what follows. But the position that had by this time been reached had fairly completely separated economic argument from any meaningful relation to externally determined norms. The scientific humanism had triumphed. And it is only now, in a cultural atmosphere of widening disenchantment, that stirrings of dissent are reaching insistent proportions.

Third, it follows from what has been said that throughout its development economics has embraced, even if not always or often in a positively articulated form, what we have referred to as immanentistic philosophic presuppositions. Immanentism is the term we have used to describe those thought systems that find their standpoint of interpretation, or their coordinating principle of explanation, somewhere within the system of reality to which that explanation is addressed. In the earlier stages of a severely individualist, introspective utilitarian theory, for example, economics embraced a fairly thoroughgoing psychologism. The mid-nineteenth-century Marxist intellectual revolt, along with other forms of collectivist thought, was established on a foundation of historicism. With the passing of extreme forms of utilitarianism and the more conscious development of empirically relevant models of the economy a pervasive materialism has characterized the subject; newer expressions of the basic ground motive of self-interest have led only to different forms of individual, class, and sectional priorities. Utilitarianism and its attendant psychologism, collectivism and its historicism, industrial-technological advance and its materialism, and now in recent times an empirically remote and largely irrelevant mathematicism have characterized the science in the last two hundred years of self-conscious development.

What these changes have meant is that once again externally provided norms of economic conduct, and of the determination of economic vision and societal responsibility, have been surrendered to a consistent economic relativism. Throughout this entire period of intellectual development the conclusion has been more widely embraced, with increasing articulateness and empirical application, that economic ends could be generally taken to justify economic and societal means. We have seen the final expression in twentieth-century materialism of a brand of economic Machiavellianism. The end, usually interpreted as the end of economic progress and the aggrandizement of class or individual gain, has been taken to justify the means. This, in turn, has led to large-scale concentrations of economic power, large concentrations of industrial and corporate power, and large concentrations of power in the hands of the suppliers of labor as transformations have occurred in the nature and rationale of trade unions. In these latter times, it has led also to large concentrations of economic power in the hands of governments. There have been, of course, countervailing groups and counter-acting pressures on all the resultant attempts of sectional interests to exploit such concentrations of power to their own advantage. But despite this resistance, the same essential feature of the system has come to consistent expression. Such external norms of economic conduct as might be expected to derive from an older ethical absolutism were surrendered to the pressures of crassly materialistic self-interest. What those norms might have been will emerge in the later sections of this chapter, where the possible

The Roots of Economic Culture

rootage of economic vision and conduct in the principles determinative of Christian thought will be briefly explored.

Fourth, there now exists an important economic dimension of what we characterized in an earlier chapter as the existentialist malaise that has descended upon us. A large part of the numbness of the social condition traces to the loss of personal identity in the presence of technological imperatives, and to a large extent man's participation in the march of a self-justifying industrialism has reduced him to the status of animate machinery. It is impossible to give an unqualified assent to the argument of Engels in his *The Origins of the Family, Private Property and the State* that "in every historical epoch the prevailing mode of economic production and exchange and the social organization necessarily following from it form the basis upon which is built and up from which alone can be explained the political and intellectual history of that epoch."[1] But it is beyond argument that forms of industrial structures, the conditions of employment, and the social formations resulting from them have had, and continue to have, considerable influence on the cultural, intellectual, and spiritual conditions that exist. To a larger extent than social criticisms have often taken care to acknowledge, what we call industrial structuration has been formative of the cultural habits, the conditions of societal relationships, and the most basic interest range and consequently the cultural orbits of large masses of people.

Although this is so, and although responsible criticism must acknowledge the influence from industrial to sociocultural formations, it would nevertheless be a mistake to conclude that the remedies for whatever is wrong reside in the collectivist class restructuring to which the statement just quoted from Engels led him. For the essential weakness of the Marxian prescription in which this concern is again being expressed most articulately at the present time is transparent. In the first place, it errs in overlooking the fact that not only is something demonstrably wrong with the condition in which we find ourselves, but that also, or even primarily, something is wrong with us ourselves. For in the last analysis we are the live and sentient actors in the drama. It is simply not true that all that is wrong with us is that we are what we are because of our circumstances, be they capitalist, or collectivist, or whatever. We are not what we are solely and simply by nurture. We are what we are, in a sense that social criticism needs fully to take into account, by nature. Something is wrong with man himself, and it is the shallowest of fallacies to imagine that his condition and status and prospects can be unalterably changed for the better simply by educating him for, or legislating for, a higher morality.

Second, it follows that the corollary weakness of the Marxian alternative is that its hopes are pinned only on social restructuration, and again no point of entry is open to externally developed norms. The mistake is that of imagining that all that is necessary to human happiness is a change in the forms of the technical mastery of nature. We are in that system of thought still locked to an ethical relativism, as we are locked to a social relativism in a thought scheme that has finally no room for absolutes of any kind at all. But we shall return to these important questions in the following chapter.

We have already seen, finally, that economics as a discipline has capitulated fairly thoroughly to the positivist methodological bequest of the natural sciences, and its so-called empirical testing partakes of the same subscription to the laws of chance that we have observed in other aspects of our intellectual tradition. In that respect, economic prescriptions and social policies are determined after inquiry at the court of the probability calculus, and programs will work, or are given a chance to work, it is thought, only as they are initially vindicated by their stance against the stochastic structures that determine them. This importation of the methodologies of the natural sciences to the human and social sciences in general, and here to economics in particular, has meant again that closer attention to externally given and absolute norms has been sacrificed to amoral probabilities, to the probabilities that the means designed will conduce to the ends envisaged. The test of rightness in economic and social affairs has too easily become that of technical efficiency, of mere mechanistic engineer-

The Roots of Economic Culture

ing, and the desiderata of humanness in what the human sciences might be conceived to be concerned with are too quickly submerged.

Thus we have a fivefold rootage of economics and economic thought and policy. In summary, we have observed (1) a continual search for a supposedly viable value-free inquiry; (2) a program of thought and analysis grounded in the assumptions of the autonomy of man himself; (3) a scheme of argument that finds its determinative presuppositions in varying forms of immanentism; (4) an economic outcome that contributes in its own way to the general formation of a materialistic, and too often a despairing, existentialism; and, finally (5) a general subscription to the same assumptions of the ultimate validity and pervasiveness of the laws of chance that, as characterized in an earlier chapter, point to the irrationalist aspect of what was there termed the rationalist-irrationalist dialecticism of contemporary thought. We shall return to other aspects of these important themes. For the present, it will be useful to look in the following sections of this chapter at the principal features of economic thought as they are determined, or are determinable, by criteria developed from Christian perspectives. In that way, we will be able to judge to what extent that uniquely theological foundation can provide a basis for genuinely sustainable economic, and thereby societal and cultural, formations.

* * *

Contemporary thought is not hospitable to the notion of creaturehood, or to that of the Creator-creature distinction in which biblical theology is grounded. Yet we have seen in an earlier discussion that it is such a nexus of thought that overarches all genuine processes of human intellection. Similarly, it is this basic construct that overarches the biblical and theologically informed perception of the economic problem. The economy and our explanation of it, as all the dimensions of our culture, stand under the sovereignty of God and in responsible relation to Him.

Therefore, as we proceed to consider the perspectives on economic culture that the Scriptures provide, we need to hold securely the derivative proposition that property as well as power reside in God. In the initial characterization of the economic problem we suggested that a most basic determinative idea was that of *conservation*. By this, it was meant that the economic problem was that of conserving the social endowment of potentially need-satisfying resources and using them in such a way as to achieve a maximum benefit for the members of the human population. But immediately it was recognized that this conception carried along with it the correlative idea or category of *stewardship,* meaning thereby that there exists a basic moral and ethical responsibility for right behavior in the allocation of resources over which we have control. This stewardship, moreover, derives its sanctions from the derivative nature of our existence and our culture under God. It is this, therefore, that now brings our initial position into coordination with the perspectives that scriptural categories provide.

The Psalmist captures the true sense of things in his summary: "The earth is the Lord's and the fulness thereof; the world, and they that dwell therein."[2] And again, "The silver is mine, and the gold is mine, saith the Lord of hosts."[3] "For every beast of the forest is mine, and the cattle upon a thousand hills."[4] The right of property carries with it the right of disposal, and in the same way the prerogative of power carries with it the prerogative of delegation. The nation of Israel was made clearly aware of these property-power relationships in the formative years following the exodus from Egypt. When the law and the divine directions were given through Moses, the promise of blessing was attached to the call for obedience. "The Lord thy God bringeth thee into a good land . . . a land wherein thou shalt eat bread without scarceness, thou shalt not lack anything in it."[5] But attached to the promise was also a warning. No man should fall into the error of concluding, "My power and the might of mine hand hath gotten me this wealth." But every man was to "remember the Lord thy God: for it is he that giveth thee power to get wealth, that he may establish his covenant which he sware unto

The Roots of Economic Culture

thy fathers." The directive was clearly addressed to the danger: "When thou hast eaten and art full, . . . Beware that thou forget not the Lord thy God. . . . Lest when thou hast . . . built goodly houses and dwelt therein: and when thy herds and thy flocks multiply, and thy silver and thy gold is multiplied, and all that thou hast is multiplied; Then thine heart be lifted up, and thou forget the Lord thy God, which brought thee forth out of the land of Egypt, . . . for it is he that giveth thee . . . wealth."[6]

At the beginning of economic thought, the scriptural data establish a threefold determinative perspective. First, all property, together with all power, resides in God, who now appears to His people not only as their Creator but as their provider and sustainer; second, God's delegation of power proceeds in parallel with his establishment of man as His responsible steward in the development of the environment in which he was placed; and third, in which the previous dimensions of thought coalesce in a new focus, it is actually God Himself who is the source and giver of wealth and of the reward for the development efforts that stewardship involves.

Here, then, is the beginning of economics in the biblical data. Man is confronted with a mandate and responsibility to work, to cultivate, and to develop. He is promised reward and success and fruitfulness in response to obedience, at the same time as he is shown that punishment and barrenness will follow disobedience.[7] But the very reward and success and the wealth they bring are not, in the last analysis, the result simply of man's working at all. The success is in a profound respect the result of the working of God. All wealth, all reward, all wages, and all economic benefits are received by those who obtain them, and are held in responsible stewardship by those who have them, because they are given to them by, and in the providence of, God Himself.

This is to be seen against the background of the curse which God placed on the ground as a result of, and as a punishment for, man's sin and his fall. The obligation of work and development did not enter as a result of sin. The ordinance of work, and in fact the ordinance explicitly of six days' labor followed by one day's rest, is a creation ordinance, the reincorporation of which into the Mosaic decalogue was explicitly accompanied by a reference back to the analogy of God's own work of creation, extending over six days and followed by a seventh day of rest.[8] Work, as enjoined on man in the original creation mandate, was therefore a blessing, a promise of fruitful participation in the activity of God. It implied the prospect that as God had created all things, so man could now enjoy the privilege of working as God's recreative steward to bring all things to the full development of their potential.

But the fact and the record of sin are only too well known. Henceforth the blessing of work would be accompanied by the pain of effort. As the entrance of sin did nothing to abrogate either the prerogative of labor or the responsibility attached to it, henceforth the labor enjoined on man was to take place in a radically new complex of conditions. The earth would give forth her fruits only after the complicating hindrances of "thorns . . . and thistles"[9] had been overcome, and the secrets and the developmental laws inherent in the created reality of the universe would yield themselves to man only after a seeming reluctance that followed a new intensity of effort on his part.

Nevertheless, it is a remarkable fact of divine providence and beneficence that the curse of the ground in the third chapter of Genesis is juxtaposed by the promise of blessing and fruitfulness as a reward for effort in the eighth chapter of Deuteronomy, just mentioned. Notwithstanding the curse and the resulting pain which effort now entails, God nevertheless gives to man those measures of understanding, skill, and ability necessary for the accomplishment of the tasks assigned to him. He implants in man the dissatisfactions provocative of developmental effort, and He provides the fruits and the rewards of the toil involved. Circumscribed as it is by the limits of the curse, and functioning within the context of the malediction on sin and evil, the providence and blessing of God nevertheless cause the demands and the purposes of His ordination with respect to the world to be brought to a full realization.

The conjunction of effort and reward needs therefore to be considered within the perspective of the providence of God. God, the scriptural data make clear, does, by the operation of His common grace, so preserve the established structure of the created order from the full decay and destruction of sin that genuine meaning and significance attach to the work and achievements even of sinful men. It is in this respect that meaning and validity adhere to the results even of apostate scientific endeavor, or scientific activity, which, rather than being directed consciously to the glory of God, proceed on the basis of the scientist's assumption of his own epistemological and metaphysical autonomy.[10] By the operation of God's common grace, significant results are achieved in the development of the created universe to the glory of God, even by men whose work proceeds on the basis of apostate postulates and principles. But, as has already been seen in a different context, full responsibility for the qualitative outcome attaches firmly to all human action. And it is not therefore possible to allow the fact of God's providential ordering of the abilities and achievements of sinful men to mitigate in any degree the rigor of the established conjunction between obedience and reward on the one hand, and disobedience and retribution on the other.

It is implied, therefore, as scriptural data confirm,[11] that God does permit wealth and prosperity to accrue to sinful men, but that He does so for a twofold purpose: first, that his own objectives of the further development of the universe might thereby be realized; and, second, that the terminal administration of God's justice may be seen to be more thoroughly vindicated, in the light of the benefits and implied responsibilities administered to men in this world. It would be a mistake to imagine that God's administration of temporal benefits implied any alleviation of the rigor of His justice, either in relation to righteousness and life on the one hand, or to sin and death on the other. The parable of Lazarus, the beggar who sat unnoticed at the gate of the rich man, serves only to underline this point.[12]

* * *

Against these concepts of the property, power, and providence of God, some principles relating to the economic organization of things appear in the earliest scriptural record. The Scriptures themselves address predominantly, of course, the unfolding in time of the purpose of God in the redemption of His people. From the initial lapse, through the historical concentration on the patriarchs, a family, a tribe, and then a nation, to the establishment of the Old Testament theocracy with its ordered structure of affairs, and on through the prophets, the captivity, and the coming at last of the promised Redeemer, the Scriptures coordinate their message on the historical accomplishment of redemption and the eventuation of all things in the interest of the church. But it would be a depreciation of the Scriptures and an inadequate hermeneutical principle to imagine that they had reference only to the affairs and the administration of the church, and that they had no direct applicability to the world and its organization outside of the church. The Scriptures do provide principles applicable to the administration of affairs in the world. The very teaching on the constitution and function of the state, for example, as distinct from the church, is adequate evidence on this point.[13]

Many principles of general economic significance derive from the law as given first through Moses and as interpreted and applied by the prophets under the Old Testament dispensation. But the earliest statement in the Scriptures of what we should now regard as having direct economic significance is actually made with reference to a situation quite outside the direct line of redemptive history. Immediately after the account of the fall and the curse, the directing and preservative grace of God comes to expression in the incorporation in society of a uniquely economic principle. This is the principle of the "specialization of economic function" and what has become known, particularly since Adam Smith's articulation of it, as the "division of labor." Essential to viable societal arrangements is the allocation to different men, to persons of different aptitudes and skill endowments, of responsibility for the performance of different economic functions. Human society is, and always has been, highly interdependent. It would be pointless and shallow to suggest that a high degree of economic interdependence awaited the emergence of advanced cultures, for example those of the large empires

The Roots of Economic Culture

of history, or the medieval manorial system that gave way to domestic manufacturers, or the guild system and a growing commercialism emanating from local trade fairs and a burgeoning international trade. It is not necessary to trace the economic history of Europe to be impressed by the necessary economic interdependence of human arrangements. Any failure to recognize the fact would follow only from a tendency to confuse the intensity or degree of realization of that principle in society with the form and inevitability of the principle itself.

When we read, therefore, that Abel was a pastoralist and Cain an agriculturalist, we are entitled to observe more in the record than the acceptability or otherwise of their offerings to God and the murder of one by the other. Again, it does not derogate from the implications or pedagogical thrust of these facts to observe in the economic specializations which Cain and Abel pursued the earliest providential structuring by God of the pattern of interdependent relations He had in view for men. Though Cain and Abel were established as a pastoralist and an agriculturalist respectively, the Psalmist reminds us again that the power of success and the fruitfulness of effort are directly attributable to God and His immanent workings in the world. "He causeth the grass to grow for the cattle, and herb for the service of man: that he may bring forth food out of the earth."[14]

Societal interdependence is a part of the created existential status in which man and human affairs have been designed and established. Economic relations, in other words, are not to be seen as primarily referable to God's redemptive design or redemptive history. The form in which economic relations come to expression is affected, as we have seen, by the fact and the working of sin. And the nature of economic relations in their institutional structure and their achievable harmony will be equally affected by the development of God's redemptive plan. But the initial reference of economic interdependence is an aspect of the created and ordained order of things, an intrinsic part of man's existential status and obligation and responsibility. The *fact* of economic arrangements is not a matter residing initially on the level of human ethics. The *form* of economic institutions and the manner of their functioning are clearly assessable against ethical mandates, but the *fact* of economic interdependence and arrangements is inherent and necessary in the ontological structure of things. The scriptural datum that "none of us liveth to himself"[15] is as clearly referable to the sphere of societal and economic interdependence as to the sphere of spiritual relationships within the church. The reason why this should be so, to anticipate a more rigorous economic argument, is that if each individual is permitted to concentrate his energies on those lines of activity for which his skill endowments are best suited and in which his productivity is accordingly greatest, the maximum total production, or "development," to use the category of the creation mandate, will tend to be achieved.

Abel, we have seen, was a "keeper of sheep."[16] After recording his death at the hand of Cain, the scriptural narrative continues to develop the history of the line of Cain, quite outside, once again, the development of redemptive history. And in this context pause is made to emphasize the building of the first city, Enoch, and the establishment of a still higher degree of economic and industrial interdependence. Abel, the keeper of sheep, is followed in this function by Jabel, "the father of such as dwell in tents, and of such as have cattle."[17] His half-brother Tubal-Cain was "an instructor of every artificer in brass and iron." And as an indication of the development of the cultural and diversionary, as distinct from the economic aspects of social arrangements, his brother Jubal "was the father of all such as handle the harp and organ."[18]

Two deductions can be made. First, this economic interdependence as an aspect of the existential structure of things brings into focus the responsibility of the individual to conserve his endowment of skills and economic resources, to develop them to their highest possible potential, and to employ them in such a way as to contribute to the development of the society's total endowment to the glory of God. The specialization of endowment and of economic function leads to the necessity of trade and the exchange of commodities produced. This interaction implies, in

The Roots of Economic Culture

turn, the responsibility of individuals to avoid such economic actions as would cause interruptions to the efficient flow of trade and to the realization thereby of the attainable societal welfare. It argues against those monopolistic concentrations of resources and power which inhibit the free and efficient circulation of goods and values and economic production.

The second of the two deductions from the basic scriptural framework relates to the need for equity, or, we may say, for nonexploitative behavior in economic relations between men. In this sense, we now see coming into view the scriptural vindication of our initial proposition that the formative principles of economics have to do, on both the personal and social levels, with the conservation of resource and skill endowments and with the development of them in such a way as to satisfy, in the context and environment of a fallen society, the demands of equity. *Conservation, development,* and *equity,* it was said, characterize the economic problem. The structure of the social and economic system is such that a free, uncluttered, and maximally beneficial circulation of resources and production is a necessary aspect of proper economic arrangements.

It might be noted that these basic notions of specialization of economic functions, interdependence, and the implications of trade, exchange, and circulation, are presented initially in Scripture without any mention of money, or of what we have come to know as the "medium of exchange." The phenomenon of money, in other words, is not of the *essence* of the economic problem. But the use of money, or the replacement of a barter economy by a monetary economy, or the facilitation of indirect exchanges—goods for money and money for goods rather than direct exchanges of goods for goods—facilitates and motivates to a high degree the very development of resources and endowments which lies at the heart of the economic problem. Many of the disorders of a complex economic system, moreover, enter precisely because of a malfunctioning of the monetary mechanism and monetary circulation.

The nature of economic affairs as part of the larger societal arrangements is confirmed and illumined further by the well-known and early scriptural record of the building of the Tower of Babel.[19] The very design and attempted implementation of the project was a denial of the obligation which the creation mandate had placed upon man. For God had originally called on men not to "build a city . . . and . . . make a name" in order to prevent, as they imagined, their being "scattered abroad upon the face of the whole earth." It was His declared wish, on the contrary, that men should disperse and that by means of the proper development of their diverse endowments they should cultivate the whole earth and subdue it to the glory of God. But two points are worthy of note in connection with this significant episode at Babel. First, the very fact that the project should be contemplated and construction could begin does itself attest the high degree of technological knowledge and industrial skill which had developed at this early time, following the reestablishment of industrial and economic culture after the Noahic flood. Even at that early date, the inhabited world had clearly enjoyed considerable development and amassed significant wealth, following the earlier stages of industrial diversification described previously. The order of God in the development of an economically interdependent culture had already proceeded to a high degree.

Second, the outcome of the Babel episode also has economic implications. For from the forcible dispersion of men which was here effected, even to the confusion and differentiation of language and the more extensive geographical distribution of population, further economic developments followed. The dispersion itself was an act of God's grace, operating in the texture of human affairs in such a way as to bring to realization the developments that, by His earliest ordination, were necessary to the ongoing cultivation of the world. And the dispersion, by establishing new degrees of the specialization of economic function and the division of labor, confirmed the necessary interdependence of separated economic entities and inhibited the evils of economically anarchic, autonomous, and unconcerned individualism or isolationism. The dispersion as opposed to concentration, moreover, pointed to the avoidance of the potentially exploitative excesses of an undue concentration of economic power. We shall return to both of these points in another context.

* * *

From this basically ordained nature of economic structures and relationships follow a large number of prescriptions for economic behavior. Although no extensive review or attempt at inductive scriptural generalization is necessary for our purposes, attention can be focused on a small number of significant and clearly observable principles.

It is clear, for example, that the distribution of economic functions did in fact give rise to an early and extensive development of trade activities. When a circumstance developed that made it desirable for the Schechemites to offer some retribution for having violated a member of the family of Jacob, the compensation proposed was largely in economic terms: "Ye shall dwell with us: and the land shall be before you; dwell and trade ye therein, and get you possession therein."[20] Joseph, it will be recalled, became prime minister and director of economic affairs in Egypt. At the height of the famine that followed the years of prosperity he invited his brothers to return and "traffick in the land."[21] And similarly, in many recorded instances, a high degree of development of commerce and economic transactions can be observed. A most eloquent passage occurs in the prophecy of Ezekiel regarding Tyrus. Here we have a picture not only of a highly developed domestic or internal trade and commerce, but also of a flourishing and prosperous international trade. This foreign trade, moreover, occurred among many nations, including the nation of Israel, and Tyrus was "a merchant of the people for many isles."[22] The extensive specialization and diversity of economic production and trade is indicated in most detailed fashion in this passage of Ezekiel's prophecy: "Judah, and the land of Israel, they were thy merchants: they traded in thy market wheat . . . and honey, and oil, and balm," and the narrative goes on to refer to trade in wine, wool, iron, clothes, sheep, spices, silver, gold, tin, brass, ivory, linen, and other items.

Here we see at the beginning of the sixth century B.C. a remarkable economic development in nations and among peoples who stand substantially outside of the mainstream of God's redemptive purpose, and we observe a pattern of smoothly functioning economic relations between them and God's chosen people. It will be clear from a glance at the long list of commodities traded, metals and manufactures as well as primary products, that the entire structure of complex and mutually advantageous trading relations was possible because God had ordained not only a distribution among different people of different skills and productive abilities, but also a unique geographical distribution of economic resources. This is the common grace of God in its uniquely economic aspect observable in one of its clearest expressions in the record of the Old Testament age.

The necessity and legitimacy of a structured set of socio-economic relationships is confirmed by the teaching of Christ and by the tenor of the New Testament ethic. We may note our Lord's cognizance of the reality of economic structures in His well-known "Render therefore unto Caesar the things which are Caesar's, and unto God the things that are God's."[23] In the parables of Christ, moreover, in those instances in which distinctively economic concepts are in view, we can observe an affirmation of the right of private property and of the responsibility of individual stewardship in the form already noted. In the parables also we find an acknowledgment and justification of free business enterprise and investment activity. But more important at present than the observation of the copious scriptural data is the precise nature of the economic ethic which is thereby brought to view. We shall refer immediately to two issues, the economic responsibility of the individual, and, as an instance of aggregative economic ethics, the question of the right attitude to the poor.

The individual, it is now clear, standing in a position of responsible stewardship under God, has been given a unique endowment of abilities and economic resources. It is a shallow myth, a misconception of humanist thought and in no sense a revelatory thought form of the Scriptures, to claim that all men are equal. It is necessary to be very clear on this point. "The

The Roots of Economic Culture

Lord," it is said, "maketh poor, and maketh rich: he bringeth low, and lifteth up."[24] It is God who is the source of all economic distinctions. "The rich and the poor meet together: the Lord is the maker of them all."[25] It is true that "with the Lord our God" there is no "respect of persons."[26] But it is necessary to distinguish two different viewpoints in this connection. First, we can observe man's status before God as a sinner, in which case all men stand on common ground by virtue of the outrage their sin has offered to the holiness of God; and, second, men stand before God in variously distributed societal functions and responsibilities. Or, to put the issue in a different form, it is true that in a sense, by virtue of their creaturehood and their sin, all men are equal before God, but God has nevertheless constituted the arrangements of human society in such a way that all men are not equal before men. Tribute is to be paid, the apostle has said, "to whom tribute is due; custom to whom custom; fear to whom fear; honour to whom honour."[27]

The first responsibility of the individual in his stewardship is to develop his personal endowments and abilities to the fullest extent possible. Diligence of effort in all aspects is clearly enjoined. "He becometh poor that dealeth with a slack hand: but the hand of the diligent maketh rich."[28] And similarly, "Servants, obey in all things your masters according to the flesh; not with eyeservice, as menpleasers, but in singleness of heart, fearing God."[29] But primarily, the responsibility of individual effort is addressed to the need for conscientious personal development, that the interests of the glory of God might thereby be more completely served. The apostolic injunctions to Timothy to "neglect not the gift that is in thee"[30] and to "stir up the gift of God which is in thee,"[31] though clearly addressed to a uniquely spiritual context of responsibility, are of a kind that applies with equal clarity and force to all aspects of individual endeavor. For it would be a strange ethic indeed that enjoined an assiduity in the cultivation of the spiritual life and permitted a slackness and indolence in any other aspect of life. To argue that such a disjunction is admissible is to misconceive the intended wholeness of life and the true rigor and integral nature of the life of the

Christian as he is called to live it in this world. It is to avoid completely the pervasive implications of the commands: "Whatsoever ye do, do all to the glory of God,"[32] and "whatsoever ye do, do it heartily, as to the Lord."[33]

The Christian man accordingly has a duty to decide carefully the limits of his physical and mental powers, to develop them in a careful and sensible manner, and to avoid all symptoms of laziness, either physical or intellectual. All this involves, of course, a reasonable mixture of work and rest, the allocation of time and resources to one's vocation, one's family, the church, and those in need. It proceeds, it is equally clear, not against the imagined standards or criteria of men, but against the demands of the precepts of God. We are to do all things, Paul has said, "to the Lord, and not unto men."[34] But the crux of the matter is that the Christian man will endeavor always to conduct himself with an observable constancy of aim and of purpose, with self-discipline and self-control. He will appreciate the need for intellectual integrity, honesty, and self-examination. It is difficult to imagine that a sound Christian witness is offered to the world by the man who is unable to work consistently and devotedly at an identified calling, except where the changes that are made in employment arise either from the need to move on to larger challenges and heavier responsibilities, or from the involuntary unemployment that may be caused by the malfunctioning of the economic system.

John Murray has made the point succinctly in his statement that "the divine ordinance is not simply that of labour; it is labour with a certain constancy,"[35] and he rightly recognizes that the ordinance of six days' labor is as insistent as that of one day's rest. Certainly there is a responsibility on the Christian to recognize that labor is a blessing as well as a duty and to be scrupulously careful in apportioning his time accordingly. If, for example, a clearer understanding of this scriptural ethic had been held, many of the industrial problems that have afflicted the economies of the Western world in recent years would have been avoided. The demand for a still shorter working week, for example, would in many instances thereby be exposed for the

The Roots of Economic Culture

hypocrisy that it is, and the dangers of moral degeneration associated with it, along with the increases in production costs and the attendant pressure to an inflationary disequilibrium in the economy, would be avoided. Paul made it clear to the Thessalonians that "if any would not work, neither should he eat,"[36] and the ethic that here comes conspicuously to view is reinforced by the same apostle's argument to Timothy that "if any provide not for his own, and specially those of his own house, he hath denied the faith, and is worse than an infidel."[37] The Christian ethic, in short, recognizing work as both a duty and a blessing, regards idleness as iniquity and finds it particularly reprehensible when idleness parades as piety, on the imagined but inadmissible grounds that scripturally prescribed work can in some sense interfere with worship and communion with God.

The Christian must therefore avoid conspicuous idleness, and he is likely to be saved from this by recognizing that his established line of employment is an endowed vocation or calling of God. In the expressive language of the Proverbs, "He that tilleth his land shall be satisfied with bread,"[38] and, "Wealth gotten by vanity shall be diminished: but he that gathereth by labour shall increase."[39] "Slothfulness casteth into a deep sleep; and an idle soul shall suffer hunger."[40] Equally clear is: "Be thou diligent to know the state of thy flocks, and look well to thy herds. For riches are not for ever,"[41] and, "He that trusteth in his riches shall fall: but the righteous shall flourish as a branch."[42] Honest and conscientious labor, in short, are enjoined by the scriptural ethic, and although riches may accrue as a blessing and reward for effort, the unwarranted dependence on riches, or the worship of them and the power they may appear to confer, are equally clearly forbidden.

The economic relationships, as well as the political relationships, that inhere in the structure of society are ordained by God in His providential ordering of the affairs of men. It is this ordering that accords a peculiar honor to every occupation that does not partake explicitly of sin.

But the scriptural principles do not imply that an inherited societal structure is necessarily, at any given time, to be regarded as being in full accordance with the preceptive law of God. To argue that they do would overlook entirely the pervasive operation in the world of the cankerous principle of sin, and the need for society continually to be returned to closer conformity to the patterns of rectitude and integrity and righteousness that God has prescribed. For society has not been redeemed, and we must necessarily address our arguments continually to the economics of a fallen society. Individual men have been redeemed, and they have been constituted by God as the "salt of the earth," the preservative against the more rapid maturation of evil and the decay of culture that sin inevitably entails. To recognize this principle implies that society needs continually to be *reformed,* and that it is to this responsible end that the Christian man has been called and appointed by God. The importance, then, of this further principle is that it ensures the avoidance by the Christian of the mistaken notion that society is to be at any point of time or at any stage ossified and that no room or mandate exists for social and economic mobility. To argue that no man should leave the economic status and function to which he was born would deny the previous principle that every man should understand honestly and develop to their full potential his particular endowments and capacities. It would deny also the Christian's responsible search for the ways in which, by possibly migrating to different economic and societal functions, always consistent, nevertheless, with the further development of his abilities, he can more completely achieve the ends to which he understands himself to be called.

It is necessary to recognize a balance and order in the scriptural economic ethic. On the one hand, the individual should enjoy a genuine opportunity for economic mobility and for personal and economic development. On the other hand, this individual mobility should always proceed in recognition of the order God has ordained. There should therefore not be any selfish or discontented usurpation of economic function by those to whom, in the ordained order of things, those functions do not properly belong. The Christian order and the Christian ethic, for example, establish that some men will be masters and some will be servants. Those who are servants, to the extent that, and so long as, God has established them as servants, are precisely instructed as to the manner in which they should conduct themselves in that capacity. Similarly, those who are masters are clearly directed as to their responsibility for fairness and equity in their relations with employees. Paul's admonition to the Colossians, for example, "Masters, give unto your servants that which is just and equal: knowing that ye also have a master in heaven,"[43] follows immediately on his corresponding injunction to servants to perform their tasks with conscientious effort and obedience. It is a basic scriptural principle that "the labourer is worthy of his hire,"[44] and the Pauline argument reflects the Old Testament prescription, "Thou shalt not defraud thy neighbor, neither rob him: the wages of him that is hired shall not abide with thee all night until the morning."[45] In fact, it is the intrusion of sin into this master-servant relationship, or, in the language of our capitalist systems, into the relations between capital and labor, that has precipitated an unduly large amount of industrial turmoil and economic dislocation. This has happened because, on the one hand, servants have wanted to behave as though they were masters, to the consequent denial of the structural order that God has ordained, and because, on the other hand, masters have avoided the apostolic injunction to justice and equity.

In the light of these principles, it would be a mistake to assume that the Scripture is opposed to capitalism as a form of economic organization. In fact, it would appear that the scriptural teaching on the right of personal property accords directly with some form of capitalist economic order, involving as it does a measure of freedom in the disposal of endowed resources and the investment of wealth, consistent with the rights of others and the ongoing development of the creation mandate. But it is clear that the scriptural teaching is opposed to the evils and injustices of which an uninhibited capitalism is capable. From all we have already seen regarding the blessing of God on obedient effort, it follows that the Christian's attitude to work will conceivably result in the acquisition of wealth, even, it is possible, in substantial increases in wealth. It would be foolhardy to imagine that the Scripture condemns wealth as such. If, as we have argued, all property resides in God, and if He is the giver of wealth and the fruits of effort, then we must clearly recognize the possibility of, and the stewardship responsibilities involved in, differential endowments of wealth. It is not the possession of money that is evil, but "the love of money" which is "the root of all evil."[46] It is not wealth that the Bible condemns, but the lust for wealth, covetousness, the vices that are all too often associated with wealth, and the misuse of whatever wealth endowment God has given. It is for this reason that Paul has argued: "Charge them that are rich in this world, that they be not highminded, nor trust in uncertain riches, but in the living God, who giveth us richly all things to enjoy; That they do good, that they be rich in good works, ready to distribute, willing to communicate; laying up in store for themselves a good foundation against the time to come, that they may lay hold on eternal life."[47]

These principles are recognized from a theological perspective by John Murray: "The economic structure presupposed in the teaching of the New Testament as well as of the Old is one in terms of the distinction between rich and poor. And it is apparent that this distinction is recognized not simply as a providential fact which the application of biblical principles would in due time eliminate, but as a distinction compatible with the divinely instituted order of society."[48] Murray further observes in this connection:

> It is simply a fact that God has not ordained equality of distribution of gift or possession. And because this is so, it is impossible to put equality into effect. Some are more capable of increasing their possessions; they are more provident, diligent, industrious, progressive. Are we to suppose that the qualities which make for the development of natural resources are to be discouraged? Are we to engage in a levelling process that will secure uniformity and make all conform to a stereotyped average? How absurd would be the attempt and how futile! Equality is not a fact of God's providence, and it is not a rule to be practiced in the order He has instituted; Diversity is a fact to be recognized and the rule to be fol-

The Roots of Economic Culture

lowed. Liberty itself must take account of inequality. Unequal distribution of wealth is indigenous to the order God has established and to the natures with which He has endowed us.[49]

Of course the evils of capitalism must be exposed and corrected, at the same time as the corrective mechanisms are not allowed to become oppressive to the point of destroying legitimate personal freedoms. Adequate scriptural evidence exists to support the conclusion that the Bible is regulative of both theory and practice in our modern economic arrangements.[50] Employer-employee relations are to be imbued with justice and equity on the one side and honest obedience and integrity of effort on the other. Differential endowments of wealth are to be expected as part of a divine ordination and are to be employed accordingly. Distinctions of economic function, orders of authority, responsibility, and obedience under equitable contracts are to be expected and preserved as part of the scripturally sanctioned order. Abuses are to be corrected, including in particular, as can be acknowledged from even a glance at the history of capitalism, abuses that impose unreasonable hardships and injustices on labor. But the righting of wrongs must not be allowed to lead only to an opposite and equally oppressive abuse. There is serious evidence at the present time, for example, that in some Western economies the earlier abuse and tyranny of capital are being allowed to give rise to a tyranny of labor, in contradiction of the scripturally sanctioned capital-labor order and relationship. As John Murray has said on this important point: "There is and has been the tyranny of the employer; that is the abuse of God-given authority. But when we have the tyranny of the servant, then we have the complete reversal of the divine order."[51] In view of the importance of this question for economic structures and their cultural implication, a further analysis and some recommendations for a sounder interpretation of the capital-labor relation will be made in the final chapter of this book.

The possession of wealth, of either a large or a small amount of wealth, imposes on the Christian the responsibility for its right disposal and use. It would not accord with the conception of stewardship, for example, for the individual who has been more liberally endowed with wealth to use it in conspicuous consumption. The good things of this world are not to be despised and are to be used legitimately and wisely by those to whom, in the providence of God, they have been entrusted. It is implicit in the scriptural directives that a man should use his resources to provide properly for his own family and to share his property sensibly in the help and encouragement of others, consistent with the command to the Galatians, for example, that "as we have therefore opportunity, let us do good unto all men, especially unto them who are of the household of faith."[52] But the dissipation of resources on needlessly flamboyant living and on an excessive indulgence in material comforts and pleasures would again not accord with the demands of Christian stewardship. When legitimate uses of wealth have been made, there will conceivably remain to the individual a certain amount of resources that can properly be employed in further economic activities. It is clear that investment by Christians in those activities that are established for the purpose of partaking explicitly in sin is prohibited. But beyond this, there are wide fields legitimately open to investment, and individual decision in this matter can be safely guided by the considerations of the conservation of property and its use for the better development of world resources to the glory of God, which we have looked at already.

The Christian, in short, will hold the things of this world lightly, remembering that "godliness with contentment is great gain. For we brought nothing into this world and it is certain we carry nothing out. And having food and raiment let us be therewith content."[53] Catherwood has observed in his characteristically insightful manner:

> The teaching of the Bible would appear to be that it is not the amount of a man's wealth which matters; what matters is the method by which he acquires it, how he uses it and his attitude of mind towards it. . . . The Christian need not live between the gasworks and the linoleum factory if he can afford to live somewhere more salubrious, but he almost

certainly should not spend three times as much as he needs on a house just because a temporary fashion has created an insatiable demand for mews and workmen's cottages in SW3. It is not necessary for the Christian woman to be dowdy, but neither is it necessary for her to order all her dresses from Paris. It is right that a Christian should want a good education for his children, but it is almost certainly wrong for him to spend money in having his children educated in purely snobbish values.[54]

It is apposite to remark, in deference to the scriptural principle of the sanctity of the individual conscience under God, that in the same way as economic effort, which may lead to the acquisition of wealth, is to be made, "not with eyeservice, as menpleasers; but in singleness of heart, fearing God,"[55] so the disposition of wealth and the exercise of stewardship over it is also to be made against the same scriptural criteria and mandates.

* * *

Economic systems, we have observed, do not necessarily function with that smooth and automatic efficiency that would guarantee the permanent provision of full employment and an even rate of economic development under conditions of maximum economic welfare. Contrary to the assumptions and propositions of the English classical economists and the industrial expansionists of the nineteenth century, there does not exist any automatic mechanism that will guarantee that a high and favorable level of the circular flow of income-generating expenditure will be maintained. It is possible, as a result, that the observed levels of expenditure, income, production, and employment may rise or fall, and in the absence of effective compensatory economic policies there may exist at any given time a larger or smaller number of involuntarily unemployed workers. Neither the economic system nor compensatory policies, monetary and fiscal policies, for example, or manpower, exchange rate, incomes, or public investment policies, may function with sufficient flexibility and efficiency to ensure that all those members of the work force willing to work and looking for a job are able to find one.

In modern economies, therefore, the existence of a certain amount of unemployment will be the rule rather than the exception. For the unemployed, depending on the length of time for which they are unemployed and the frequency with which they find themselves in that condition, this will mean a greater or lesser degree of poverty, the torture of economic anxiety, and the humiliation of economic distress. Poverty may therefore result from a chronic or unexpected malfunctioning of the economic system, or from a failure of the system to adjust sufficiently rapidly to changes in the economic environment and variations in the demands for commodities and employment.

The amount of employment that can be offered in certain industries or in certain regions of the country may decline for other reasons also. There may be a permanent movement of demand away from the products of an industry onto substitute commodities, or a change in technology and industrial processes may render certain commodities or materials obsolete. A movement of demand from, say, horse-drawn carriages to automobiles could give rise to such so-called technological unemployment. Or indeed, the same phenomenon could result to some extent simply from a fairly rapid and large-scale movement of demand from large to small automobiles, particularly if, as has happened in recent years in the United States, the demand for small cars is a demand for imported rather than home-produced vehicles. In the material inputs to production processes, a movement away from a principal reliance on coal as a source of energy, for example, and the adoption of competing forms of fuel supply may give rise to chronic unemployment in previously active coal-producing regions, such as Appalachia in the United States. In such a case, the involuntary unemployment that results can be said to be structural rather than cyclical, and a quite different set of counteracting economic policies may be necessary to deal with it. Unemployment and poverty may be due also to discrimination in the economic system, against racial or religious minorities for example, or from deliberate policies of the restrictions of supplies and of employment opportunities, such as may arise from monopolistic industrial behavior.

The Roots of Economic Culture

But for whatever reason it may occur, the economic system may be confronted from time to time, and more or less continually in varying degrees, with the problem of unemployment and poverty. There are more reasons than might often have been imagined to give credence and point to our Lord's observation that "ye have the poor always with you."[56] It is a remarkable fact that after poverty and the state of the poor were accorded such a high prominence in the explicit articulation of the Christian ethic, after centuries of observation of the relatively depressed economic status of the masses of the people, and after, in particular, the jarring disturbances in economic advance during the past two hundred years of the industrial and scientific revolution, it should have taken so long for a sound apprehension of the causal economic reasons for poverty to emerge. It will be useful at this point to fill out the scriptural background of this concern.

It was a particularly embracive dictum of the writer of the Proverbs that "when the righteous are in authority, the people rejoice: but when the wicked beareth rule, the people mourn."[57] But the particular focus to which the statement was directed, like that of many comparable arguments of both Testaments, was that of the condition and status of the poor: "The righteous considereth the cause of the poor: but the wicked regardeth not to know it,"[58] and, "The poor and the deceitful man meet together: the Lord lighteth both their eyes. The king that faithfully judgeth the poor, his throne shall be established for ever."[59] Many of the situations in which the ethics of the attitude to the poor was adduced had to do with loans of money and commodities to those in conditions of extreme need or near destitution. It was in this context that the question and problem of usury arose. "The rich ruleth over the poor, and the borrower is servant to the lender."[60] The question of usury, or the rate of interest, appears to have fascinated most historians of economic thought, no doubt in large part because of the casuistry that surrounded the topic in the medieval church. This occurred as Thomist ethics wrestled to release business investment of money capital from the Aristotelian dictum that "money is barren" and that therefore money lent could not properly earn money. The issue, unfortunately, has not been clearly understood, and it will be useful to look at the main considerations involved.

Usury, clearly, was prohibited under the Mosaic law: "If thou lend money to any of my people that is poor by thee, thou shalt not be to him as a usurer, neither shalt thou lay upon him usury."[61] Interest on loans in such cases was quite simply not to be charged at all. The point to be grasped, however, is that the prohibition of interest has reference simply to loans to the poor, which means loans to relieve their distress, and the commandment is broadened in an interesting fashion in the Deuteronomic statement of the law: "Thou shalt not lend upon usury to thy brother; usury of money, usury of victuals, usury of any thing that is lent upon usury: Unto a stranger thou mayest lend upon usury."[62] The situation is perhaps best clarified in G. Ernest Wright's comment on this last passage: "No interest is to be charged on loans to a fellow Israelite, though it is permissible in the case of a foreigner. Since most loans in Israel were for the purpose of relieving distress, the principle behind the law was that another's need should not be the occasion for profit. The use of loans in international commerce was for another purpose. Hence the foreigner is excluded from the requirement."[63] Although this explanation considerably clarifies the issue, it affords also a scriptural foundation to what was noted earlier as an international specialization of economic production, division of labor, and trade. Calvin, we shall see later, released the question of interest on loans from the casuistry that surrounded it in the medieval church and brought the problem into the clear air of the reasonableness of rates of return on loans for business investment.

Thus a significant aspect of the Old Testament ethic is its continuing concern for the state and condition of the poor. A similar concern must underlie a more fully developed economic ethic in the complex societal structures of the present time. It is against the background of the precepts just examined that the writer of the Proverbs says, "He that hath pity upon the poor lendeth unto the Lord; and that which he hath given will he pay him again."[64] Moreover, the reinterpretation of the Old Testa-

The Roots of Economic Culture

ment ethic in the teaching and parables of our Lord has left a similar deposit of concern for the poor. Familiarity with the New Testament teaching and history makes it unnecessary to expand the question further at this point, but it can be noted that the parables of Christ do bear in certain other interesting ways on some issues we have already raised.

Consider first the parable of the pounds in Luke, chapter 19, which, for the purposes of the points to be made here, is closely parallel with the parable of the talents in the twenty-fifth chapter of Matthew's Gospel. The parables indicate the right of the individual to earn a rate of return on the business investment of money capital and, indeed, a responsibility to invest wisely, important spiritual lessons being taught by means of this precise analogy. In both cases, punishment was inflicted on those stewards who had not improved their opportunities and who did not put their endowments to profitable and productive uses. Here is a significant linkage in the teaching of our Lord with the Old Testament precepts that conjoined diligence and reward on the one hand, and slothfulness and punishment in God's providence on the other.

The parables, of course, were designed to teach highly significant spiritual lessons, and a proper understanding of them requires a rigorous concentration on the single principal lesson in view. It is an improper exegetical method to endeavor to discover parallel applications in the realm of the spiritual life of all of the details in the parables. They did, however, repeatedly invoke the analogies of everyday situations and life patterns with which the hearers would be familiar, and it is therefore appropriate to consider for our present purposes the principal thrust of the analogies on which they are based. With this in mind, we can refer also to the parable of the hired servants, or laborers in the vineyard, reported in the twentieth chapter of Matthew's Gospel. It will be recalled that in the outcome those laborers who were hired in the eleventh hour of the day received the same payment as that for which the workers hired at the beginning of the day had contracted. Leaving aside the theological question that here the sovereignty of God in the distribution of the benefits of redemption comes forcibly into view, the perspective established by the analogy employed is of some significance. We have seen that the previous parable established by analogy the legitimacy and propriety of return on business investment, and in the present case the analogy establishes the economic right of freedom of contract in business activity. As in the case of the spiritual application, the details need not be pressed in establishing the empirical validity of certain actions in the economic sphere from which, so frequently, our Lord chose the simple analogies He put to such profoundly important use.

* * *

To this point, we have raised a number of concepts foundational to economic analysis—interpersonal and interregional differences in resource endowments, specialization of economic functions, division of labor, interregional and international trade, exchange, wealth, poverty, property, consumption, and investment. These coalesce in the important concept of the circulation throughout the healthy economy of resources and commodities, economic values, and wealth. It follows from what has been said that material goods are instruments of God's providence.[65] Those individuals who have been placed in possession of larger amounts of resources or wealth are required to recognize their possessions as such and to realize that in the general case the resources themselves and the economic values and activity-creating potential within them cannot confer any benefit upon society unless they are made to circulate. Wealth, therefore, acquires its legitimacy only to the extent to which it is employed or circulated for the benefit of society at large. It is possible to see from these larger perspectives the elements of truth in the eighteenth-century arguments that the expenditure of the rich conferred economic benefits on the poor, and in the fear of John Locke in the seventeenth century that "the money of the nation may lie dead, and thereby prejudice trade."

The unequal distribution of wealth and resources and the divinely ordained distinctions between the rich and the poor now come into clearer perspective. For if there is reason to believe that our initial argument is correct, that the societal and economic structures are, *as to their basically interdependent forms,* part of the existentially ordained structure of affairs, an important implication follows. The responsibility for the development of the world required by the creation mandate cannot be discharged unless the resources and wealth, wherever they are at any time located, are actually put to work and employed in an optimal fashion. This, in short, is the expression in the economic sphere of the basic fact of human solidarity, a datum that comes to expression in many ways in God's administration of human affairs. It is therefore not overstating the case to say that "the rich man has a providential economic mission."[66] This mission is not exhausted by, or even principally concerned with, the scriptural commands to charity and liberality. The rich, rather, serve the interests of the poor in a more indirect but ultimately beneficial way. They do so by the judicious employment of their wealth in the generation of economic activity, employment, and more widely generalized prosperity and development. It is the danger of failing to recognize the obligations that lie in these directions that constitutes in a significant sense the snare of riches. Wealth is to be conserved and sensibly employed, and it is the awareness of that stewardship that is calculated to preserve the owners of wealth from the danger just adduced.

John Calvin understood the structure and functioning of economic relationships in terms such as these. He had no confidence in the ability of an unfettered individualism to produce automatically an economic harmony, and he therefore understood the overall mission of the state to involve an intervention where necessary in economic affairs. Sin, Calvin saw, vitiated all of human actions, and it introduced a massive disorder into society. It was therefore necessary for the state, being ordained by God for the restraint and correction of evil, to take action when necessary to deal with the expression and fruits of sin, as much in the economic as in other realms of society. Albert Hyma records, for example, in his valuable *Renaissance to Reformation,* that "in the winter of 1544-1545, Calvin appeared before the city Council of Geneva, and urged the magistrates to find work for the unemployed. Living as he did in the midst of an urban population, he saw about him a large number of paupers who were willing to work, but who could not find employment. It is to be doubted that such unhappy conditions increased Calvin's respect for life in the cities. On the other hand, he could not help himself from showing continued interest in industrial employment which provided many members of his church with their only source of income."[67] Calvin saw that if the state did not intervene in appropriate circumstances, even, as in the case just noted, to provide work and therefore income for the unemployed, the malfunctioning of the economic system would introduce obstructions to the circulation of goods and wealth. This would cause a waste, rather than a conservation, of endowed resources, to the neglect of the ongoing development for which the creation mandate made society responsible.

This danger of obstructions to the circulation of wealth and resources Calvin saw also in the fact that "usually the merchants, through their astuteness and artifices, attract to themselves the greater part of the world's wealth . . . they enrich themselves through their fraud and their illicit and evil trade."[68] In the same way, he complained against the restrictive speculative hoarding by merchants who would "rather let the grain spoil in their bins than sell it to people when they need it,"[69] and he therefore attacked those who, by such means, artificially caused prices to rise in order to increase their profits. The same clogging interruptions to a smooth functioning of economic relations Calvin saw in the complaint of the prophet Amos against those who "swallow up the needy, even to make the poor of the land to fail, saying, When will the new moon be gone, that we may sell corn? and the sabbath that we may set forth wheat, making the ephah small and the shekel great, and falsifying the balances by deceit? That we may buy the poor for silver, and the needy for a pair of shoes; yea, and sell the refuse of the wheat."[70] Calvin refers to Amos's exposure of "the avarice of the rich, who in time of scarcity held the poor subject to themselves and reduced them to slavery."[71] The basic complaint is akin to that of the

The Roots of Economic Culture 113

prophet Isaiah against unlawful and economically damaging monopolies: "Woe to them that join house to house, that lay field to field, till there be no place, that they may be placed alone in the midst of the earth."[72] The desire for monopoly ownership was motivated again by the desire for inordinate profit and riches, which depended, in turn, on the improper exploitation in economic affairs of those with whom transactions were effected.

Only too easily, it has been seen, money, which God in His providence has established as the means by which the wealth and resources of the economy can be circulated, can itself become a god. In this sense, money, the circulation of which makes possible the conversion of wealth from one form to another, does, as André Biéler has said, put man to a test.[73] Money can take "the place of God in the heart of sinful man."[74]

> The victory of Mammon over man does not produce only the crookedness of the individual; it immediately also brings about the perversion of society and church. Immense perturbations follow in economic life, engendering social disorder. Selfish appropriation of wealth, hoarding, cornering, monopolization, greed, and avarice as well as waste, prodigality, luxury, or absense of sobriety—visible expressions of sin—block the harmonious circulation of goods foreseen in God's order. These disorders falsify the just repartition and distribution of money within creation according to the purpose of God. They clog an equitable redistribution of the benefits of wealth among all.[75]

Calvin also, as noted earlier, released the question of usury from the casuistry in which the medieval church had enveloped it. For Calvin, a reasonable rate of interest on business loans was entirely acceptable, and a rate of return on money capital adequate to motivate its employment in legitimate business activity was to be expected. Money, Aristotle had urged, was barren, and income could not therefore properly be earned from the lending of money. We have already seen, of course, that this empty argument is directly contradicted by the Deuteronomic statement of the law against usury, and it has been clarified also by the analogical content of certain of the parables of our Lord.

It is a remarkable fact that confusion in economic thought should have surrounded this question for as long as it did. In view of the significance of money capital and its productive economic employment, the following comment of Calvin might be noted:

> Money lying in a box does not beget money. There it is indeed sterile. And no one will borrow money unless he intends to work with it. That is because the profit is not made with the money itself but with its revenue. . . . The problem will be made clearer by using an example. There is a certain rich man who has plenty of property and income but no cash at the moment. There is another person who owns less property and has less income but happens to possess more cash. The first party goes to the second and asks for a loan and offers some of his property as security. The security or mortgage renders the loan more permissible and acceptable than other loans.[76]

The context here refers not to consumption loans made by one Israelite to another who found himself in a situation of distress. The reference is to ordinary commercial enterprise and business transactions, and, subject to the overriding conditions of fairness and equity in such dealings, there were no reasons why such loans should not be made and a reasonable rate of interest received. Indeed, there was every reason why such loans should be made, as a means, implicit in this example of Calvin's, of making possible the active and beneficial circulation of wealth in the manner in which we have just considered it.

A larger examination of the economic thought of Calvin than can be undertaken at this time would reveal a comparable clarity of insight on a number of issues analogous to the many that confront the economist and the economic policy maker in these modern times. Proposals for the creation of new industrial activities in Geneva, as a means of putting the unemployed to work, can be found in his writings, together with proposals regarding labor and salary contracts, legal arbitration of industrial disputes, and price control on temporarily scarce necessities. He argued also against the widespread trade practices of monopolistic control of the supplies of certain commodities and the con-

The Roots of Economic Culture 115

sequent excess profiteering from the practice of price discrimination. Perhaps a principal thrust of Calvin's economic concern, one that brings it into consonance with our own theses in this book, is contained in his comment on the text of James: "Behold, the hire of the labourers who have reaped down your fields, which is of you kept back by fraud, crieth: and the cries of them which have reaped have entered into the ears of the Lord of sabaoth."[77] "What greater violence can we find," Calvin writes, "than that by which hunger and poverty starves those who feed us by their labour? And yet such a strange cruelty is quite common. For, many men have a tyrannical nature and think that mankind has been made only for them. . . . We must note that Saint James adds that the cry of the poor reaches up to the ears of God so that we may know that the wrongs done to the poor will not remain unpunished."[78]

Economics in a Christian perspective must similarly be concerned with what Calvin called the "strange cruelty" suffered by those who, for one reason or another, are economically disadvantaged, or are unable to protect themselves against the hardships and injustices meted out to them by the malfunctioning of the economic system. We should be concerned not only with Calvin's "hunger and poverty," such as results from the unemployment which the unfettered working of the economic system can generate from time to time, but also with the problem of inflation as well as deflation and with the erosion of economic values, wealth, and property by the excessively rapid rise in prices that characterizes inflationary conditions.

But that, of course, conceptualizes rather than solves our problem. It would be necessary, in a larger work on economic policies and in an argument directed primarily to that objective, to consider at some length the structures and responsibilities of economic policy-making bodies, such as those of the state, for example, which will be referred to again in the next chapter. This, moreover, would return our argument to a point at which we began. For to envisage the existence of a more or less centralized economic policy-making body that has legitimate functions to perform is to acknowledge that, as recognized in our critique of classical and neoclassical economic thought, we have no confidence that if left to itself a complex economic system will automatically equilibrate at a condition of high employment, generalized prosperity, and maximum economic welfare.

Calvin, it can be shown, wrote substantially from the background of very similar concerns. A conclusion from Biéler's study of Calvin's economic thought is apposite: "There is no doubt that Calvin's emphasis on personal responsibility would never have led him to ask the state to be the exclusive animator of economy. Yet Calvin's awareness of the ambiguity of man's nature (that is, of the plain fact that man is consistently solicited by both God and Mammon) would never have inclined Calvin to believe that society can reach a harmonious economic activity through the simple play of individual interests."[79] The perspective against which the economic problem comes to expression is provided not only by the considerations of creaturehood and finitude, but also, it has now been adequately seen, of sin. It is from directions such as these that a distinctively theological perspective, and in particular the viewpoint of scriptural Christianity, are brought to bear on the economic problem and through that on the larger questions of our societal and cultural structures.

6

Economics, Culture, and Rationality

It is beyond the scope of our present objectives to attempt the construction of either an extensive theology on the one hand or a more detailed theoretical and applied economics on the other. Our task has been the more modest one of bringing into focus some of the principal thought forms and categories of analysis that theology and economics bring to the critique of our cultural condition. In particular, it is important at this time to observe the manner in which economics and Christian belief are connected and interrelated and how they together raise questions whose resolution or proper explication have social and cultural significance. In the preceding chapters, considerable progress has been made in this direction. We have sketched some of the main lines of the contemporary intellectual climate, the sociocultural deposit of a widespread existentialism, the perspectives that economists generally command in their analysis of the scheme of things, and the biblico-Christian framework within which desiderata and sanctions of economics might be seen. In the present chapter, and again within the fairly circumscribed limits we have set, a number of the most important implications of the analysis to this point will be examined.

Though it is not necessary to rehearse the argument in detail, and though we shall extract in what follows only a small number of their more direct implications, it will be useful to bear in mind the propositions in terms of which we have summarized the rootage of economic thought and policy. We have observed that economics as it developed to maturity as an intellectual discipline became involved in a search for a supposedly value-free inquiry; that it erected a framework of thought and analysis grounded in the contemporary philosophic and methodological assumptions of the autonomy of man himself; that it led in large degree to a generalized materialism which, by and large, excluded any point of entry for externally derived norms and ethical criteria; that in doing so it embraced varying forms of immanentism, for example, psychologism, historicism, and mathematicism; and that in all this it depended for its epistemological self-consciousness on assumptions of the ultimate validity and pervasiveness of the laws of chance. It was these latter, we observed, that pointed to the irrationalist aspect of what we termed the rationalist-irrationalist dialecticism of contemporary thought.

Against this background, the remaining discussion can best proceed in terms of a small number of dichotomous guidelines, the parts of which stand either in tension or in correlation with each other. In each case, moreover, the full understanding of their significance and their contribution to a social and cultural critique turns on the extent to which they are illumined by the categories of Christian thought already raised.

The questions that now arise can be summarized under the headings of (1) the meaning and distribution in society of property and power; (2) the determinants and prospects of economic stability and growth, or the secure realization of current benefits on the one hand, and the expansion of future satisfaction on the other; (3) the tensions, the pressing realities and existential tensions, between freedom and security; (4) the correlation between economic and social responsibilities and benefits; and (5) the simultaneous realization of equity and opportunity. A number of cognate issues, for example the economic prerogatives and responsibilities of the state, the relevance to the arguments of certain current claims of collectivism and capitalism, motivations of individual and social behavior, and the apparent grounding of these and related matters in social theory will be referred to.

* * *

Economics, Culture, and Rationality 119

We recall, first, that economics, as argued in our introductory analysis of the epistemological scope of the subject, is not, and cannot be, a value-free inquiry. The economist necessarily brings to his task the same kind of pretheoretical commitment or prescientific philosophic persuasion as is naturally brought to every field of investigative inquiry. In the present case, the pretheoretical commitments that exist preclude us from discovering the legitimate starting point for economic inquiry in claims for individualism or collectivism, or for capitalism or socialism. For behind the interesting and important dichotomies that here come into view lie deeper springs of human action and deeper motivations and ethical responsibilities. If, moreover, these are not recognized, economic and social thought become quickly locked in a fruitless immanentism and are mired in the pointless circularity that their intramundane postulates produce. Sustainable meaning, we have argued on the contrary, inheres only in a thought system that takes as its starting point the postulate of the Creator-creature distinction, and that finds its final reference point and locus of predication in God and His ordering of possibilities, and in His establishment of the apparently contingent space-time actualities that exist.

As economics has developed and brought its weight to bear on social and cultural formations, it has capitulated heavily to markedly positivist and scientistic categories. This has remained substantially the case, though we can observe in later times something of a faltering and an uncertainty of direction and an asking of new questions pointed to not so easily quantifiable problems of human welfare. New concerns are arising about the distribution among classes and among nations of the achievable benefits on a global scale of what economic advance can produce. But the critical issue for our present purposes is that in its methodological uneasiness and in its partially disturbed conscience on matters of economic ethics, economics in general, to take the conclusion of Joan Robinson's *Economic Philosophy* as a modern benchmark, has brought us only to a generalized agnosticism. Christian consciences will not easily subscribe to Robinson's ethical nihilism in her conclusion that "the moral problem is a conflict that can never be settled. Social life will always present mankind with a choice of evils. No metaphysical solution that can ever be formulated will seem satisfactory for long. The solutions offered by economists were no less delusory than those of the theologians that they displaced." Nor can we see much radiance in the seemingly pointless gesture: "All the same we must not abandon . . . hope."[1]

It is not that the Christian economist must perforce award higher marks than Joan Robinson is prepared to give to the ethics, the methodologies, and the knowledge constructs of the nineteenth- and twentieth-century economists who have substantially structured the discipline. Quite to the contrary, we have looked already at the philosophic assumptions and persuasions of the statesmen of the profession themselves—Smith, Mill, Sidgwick, Marshall, and Keynes, for example—and we have observed in some instances a conscious, deliberate, and articulate recantation from earlier and professedly Christian positions. We have noted the long journey and the theologico-philosophic devolution from the first edition of Adam Smith's *Moral Sentiments* at the end of the eighteenth century to the brilliant exposure of the economists' philosophic predilections in Keynes's *Essays in Biography* in the middle of the twentieth century.

When we look at the possible explanatory significance of the classical notions of "self-interest," on the one hand, and "happiness" and its offspring of "utility," on the other, we can observe a coalescence of viewpoint. These concepts have converged in a quasi-moralistic justification of the arguments for laissez-faire in economic thought and policy. It was not that a full-fledged economic or social condition of laissez-faire could be, or ever was, realized in fact. The discordant realities of the world kept all too obviously getting in the way. Uncertainties, ambivalences, and changes of thought direction occurred between the "economic harmony" postulates of Adam Smith's "hidden hand" theorizing and the Benthamite interventionist argument that the mythical harmonies were neither realistic in theory nor observable in fact. But there has been throughout the nineteenth century and down to the present time, notwithstanding the historical testimony of slump and inflation and depression and boom, a yearning for the intellectual simplicities of the laissez-faire theory, and for an espousal of the economic proposition that that government governs best which governs least. It is doubly disturbing that confidence in the imagined aggregative harmonies in the economic system, and in the assumptions of an automatic full-employment reequilibrating mechanism in economic society, should in recent times have begun to be claimed again by avowedly Christian economists.

We have seen human action vitiated by sin, and we have seen what might be called a double disequilibration in the economic system. First, the economic system is shot through with natural pressures to dislocation and disequilibrium—swings of business confidence, investment and financial market interdependencies, instabilities of capital formation, the danger of monetary mismanagement, wage determination rigidities, and restrictive industrial practices—which make it the normal and expected state of affairs that the level of expenditures, production, incomes, and employment in the economy will fluctuate. But superimposed on these natural tendencies to disequilibrium and instability is the second disequilibrating pressure, an all-too-frequent manifestation in economic affairs of the exploitation, to the disruption and disadvantage of society as a whole, of the excessive concentration of economic power.

Such concentrations of economic power have frequently occurred in the past, particularly during the nineteenth- and early twentieth-century sweep of the industrial revolution, in the hands of industrialists and monopolistic, or oligopolistic, industrial firms. And there is need for caution in this day lest raw monopoly power should again be allowed to exploit workers, consumers, suppliers, and society. But the particular point at which the worrying dangers of monopolistic exploitation confront us today is at the point of concentration of economic power in the hands of the trade unions. This, moreover, has deeper implications for societal stability and for the need to bring societal structures back to conformity with scriptural constructs. We have seen the theologian John Murray speak soberly but with disturbingly sure insight: "There is evidence that we are heading at a disquieting pace for reversal of what we must call the biblical economy. If we have not arrived we are on the verge of arriving at the mastery of labor, and that means the tyranny of labor. There is and has been the tyranny of the employer; that is the abuse of God-given authority. But when we have the tyranny of the servant, then we have the complete reversal of divine order."[2]

It is not that we have argued at any point for an ossification of social and economic structures or for the consolidation at any time of the economic status quo, so that no opportunities or scope for economic mobility existed. Quite to the contrary, we have called for maximum efforts at individual personal development and for opportunities for a maximum freedom of economic and occupational migration. But we have at the same time recognized the clear biblical ethic governing relations between masters and servants, calling for diligence of effort by servants, to the extent that, and for so long as, they are established by God as servants, and for the just and equitable treatment of servants by masters, to the extent that they are established by God as masters. We have argued firmly against the unlawful usurpation of economic functions by those to whom, in the providence of God, those functions have not at that specific time been distributed.

In the outcome, a Christian perspective on the economic problem will necessarily fragment into a number of operational objectives in the kind of mixed capitalist economies with which we are familiar in the Western democracies. Without anticipating any detail at all at this point, it is possible to set against these operational objectives a range of legitimate economic policy instruments and options. These can properly be seen as potentially contributing to the fuller realization of the economic obligations imposed on man by the creation mandate, at the same time as scriptural desiderata of personal freedom and dignities are preserved. The inevitability of fluctuations in the economic system imposes on the Christian economic conscience the need to understand the real nature of causation in the economic structures of the fallen society and to understand also the limits and scope, the potential and advisability, of contracyclical, compensatory economic policy actions.

* * *

No question conducts us more rapidly to the heart of the economic problem, or brings the societal relevance of the subject more pointedly to focus, than that of the ownership of property and the distribution of power that property implies. This is again determining the thrust of the new radicalism on the political and social left, as it is hardening the stance of what is the new and articulate right. Marxism, we have had cause to notice, is again alive and thriving in contemporary debates on social and economic issues. New forms of class consciousness clamor for recognition as reputable spokesmen for desirable social policies. New claims for the legitimacy of the "class struggle," unable to claim homogeneity of either perspective or purpose but sharing a common persuasion that the ills of our culture lie at the door of a now decadent capitalism, are boasting new and widening allegiances. In their argument for a new "participatory form of socialism," for example, Professors Richard C. Edwards, Michael Reich, and Thomas E. Weisskopf, as representatives of the new radicalism, present us with a vision of human nature, its educability, its essential goodness, and its apparent perfectibility, that harks back to the claims of the earlier post-Enlightenment optimism. "Our vision of a radical transformation of the United States," they observe, "clearly involves far more than formal changes in political and economic institutions. Such changes must be part of an ongoing process of change in social and cultural consciousness that will constitute a revolution of social relations among people."[3] It is clear that these authors' concern focuses on precisely the same questions as have motivated our discussion throughout this book. But their statement continues in a way that not only stands in polar opposition to the perspectives of Christian thought we have already proposed, but evinces a cultural and an anthropological grounding that can hardly sustain the weight of the argument they place upon it: "We do *not* regard men and women as inherently greedy, acquisitive, selfish, competitive, or aggressive. Human nature has shown enormous variation in time and space, and it seems to be in large part a product of the social environment. We believe that changes in the environment can interact with changes in the individual to usher in a new era of human cooperation." (*See* Chapter 6, Note 3.)

This statement is worthy of note because it is an unusually candid and forthright example of the philosophic basis underlying many of the claims of the new radicalism. It betrays the same humanistic orientation and dependence on assumptions of human potential that informed earlier strands of optimistic thought. Indeed, the forms in which the claims of libertarianism on the one hand and collectivism on the other have come to expression during the last hundred years have been mainly the markings of the swinging pendulum of natural law and humanistic assumptions. Man, in one way or another, has been imagined to be the master of his fate. New forms of what we have noted as social and economic engineering have come into vogue, and now we see as the unabashed claim at the philosophic foundation of social and cultural recommendations that morality after all can be legislated. It is claimed that ethical rectitude can be educated, and changes in environment are adequate for the perfection of human nature. Quite apart from the antithetical categories of Christian thought, all this is a far cry from Shakespeare's dictum, "The fault, dear Brutus, is not in our stars but in ourselves."[4]

Claims to property, whether made in terms of the right of private ownership, the legitimacy of democratic or participatory socialism, or the vesting of ownership in the state or in statutory or political agencies, must all be examined against the fact that property and power reside in God. This we have seen coming to expression in various ways in the preceding chapter. The Psalmist has put the issue in poetic form: "For every beast of the forest is mine, and the cattle upon a thousand hills."[5] And "The earth is the Lord's, and the fulness thereof; the world, and they that dwell therein."[6] This fact, moreover, grounded the covenantal relations between God and His people in that early theocratic state in which they were established after the exodus from Egypt.

"Thou shalt remember the Lord thy God: for it is he that giveth thee power to get wealth, that he may establish his covenant which he sware unto thy fathers."[7]

Property, we have seen, carries with it the prerogative of distribution, and power implies the right of delegation. The Creator-creature distinction that underlies the Christian perspective on social thought implies that property rights exist as derivative, and that they are distributed and sustained by the works of providence by which God's purposes in the world are executed. The manner in which this basic datum influenced the earliest theocratic structure of things can be exemplified, without the need for any extensive examination, by reference to the law of land ownership and sale. The twenty-fifth chapter of Leviticus, from which the well-known statement inscribed on the Liberty Bell in Philadelphia is taken, "Proclaim liberty throughout all the land unto all the inhabitants thereof,"[8] sets out the regulations covering the "year of jubilee." At that time, which was to occur every fifty years, all land was to return to the ownership of the person to whom it had originally been granted. "The land shall not be sold for ever," the text stated, "for the land is mine."[9] Between the years of jubilee the land could not be sold outright and in perpetuity, but only the *use* of the land could be sold. A carefully stated set of economic regulations, moreover, came into effect at the same time. The price at which the use of the land was to be sold at any time was to be determined by the number of years remaining from the purchase date to the "year of . . . jubilee" on which "ye shall return every man unto his possession." As to the sale price, therefore, "according to the multitude of years thou shalt increase the price thereof, and according to the fewness of the years thou shalt diminish the price of it; for according to the number of years of the fruits doth he sell unto thee."[10]

To interpret the significance of this dictum for our present-day social and economic structures, it is necessary to keep clearly in mind one important fact, the oversight of which has unfortunately misled a number of Christian commentators in recent times. This is the fact that the data we have just inspected referred directly to the theocratic state and relationships in which the people of God to whom they were addressed at that time existed. But it is all too clear, from a proper understanding of the development of God's purpose and His administration of His purposes in history and in the world, that we do not live at this time in a theocracy in the sense in which that was previously the case. In those earlier times, the Israelite nation was the church, "the church in the wilderness,"[11] and in that sense and capacity it constituted also the theocracy. Its sociocultural and economic relations were constructed accordingly. Correspondingly, the Christian church is now the nation, "an holy nation,"[12] and extreme care must be exercised in prescribing at the present time sanctions and desiderata applicable to the church, on the one hand, and the world outside the church, on the other.

We do not live in a theocracy at this time. We live, quite simply, in a fallen society. Whatever we have to say about economic and cultural prescriptions for society must be said about that fallen society. Sin, all too clearly, is abroad in the world and in the hearts of men. Our economics, it should be equally clear, must be the economics of a fallen society, with all the proclivities to disharmony and to disequilibrium discussed already. It should be borne in mind, of course, that the moral law is inviolate, and on the sanctity and perpetuity of that law of God we should rightly insist. But that in no sense permits the conclusion that normative significance attaches at this time to the precise forms, and to the societal and institutional arrangements, in which the administration of the law first came to expression. The latter, it becomes clear on inspection, were determined by the precise structure of civil laws, which, in the context in which they were first promulgated, were designed to bring to societal and cultural focus the spiritual demands of the moral law itself.

The translation to a contemporary societal norm of the Levitical law of property and the arrangemens for the year of jubilee turns on the injunction that law contained: "If thou sell ought unto thy neighbour, or buyest ought of thy neighbours's hand, ye shall not oppress one another."[13] In other words, we see coming to focus the general insistence on equity in economic and social transactions and arrangements. Equity, we suggested earlier, was, along with conservation and development, one of the basic coordinating concepts under which the meaning and relevance of economics was to be explored.

The biblical data permit and require the institution in society of private property. This is clear from the decalogue, where the sanctity of private property is protected in particular by the eighth and tenth commandments: "Thou shalt not steal" and "Thou shalt not covet."[14] Moreover, if cogency attaches to our argument that the Creator-creature distinction establishes the derivative nature of all property rights and the assumption of power that accompanies them, then this brings into prominence again the other foundational rubric with which we began, namely, the notion of stewardship. In the constitution of human societies, these very data establish an intensely individual and personal relation and obligation between God and man. Stewardship is basically individual. And it is for their individual stewardship that men are, and will be, held accountable. It is this that points to the deficiencies and the ethical weaknesses of many of the arguments for the transfer to the state and statutory bodies of the ownership rights and responsibilities otherwise vested in individuals.

The various forms of collectivism, of course, and in particular the new forms of Marxist-inspired radicalism that have lately come into vogue, argue as a basic tenet of their systems that private property should in due course be abolished and resource ownership be vested in the state. We must look, it is said, to the eventual demise of capitalism and to its replacement by variously described forms of collective ownership. This, in turn, is argued on grounds similar in many respects to what we have just elevated as equity in societal arrangements, and on grounds, in many of its forms, of strongly perceived and articulated class interests. The so-called class struggle is, in these views, very much alive, and it is the task of properly conceived social analysis to keep it alive in the interests of the eventual rearrangement and realignment of those class relationships. The detail need not detain us at this point. Indeed, the detail does vary from one form of radical social theorizing to another. What is important for the present is the relevance of the argument for what we have advanced as the alternative and antithetical Christian perspective on the property-power relationship.

Marxism is, we have argued, by the very nature of its atheistic grounding and its atheological analytical processes, a closed system. It is, to employ our earlier term, immanentistic. No extensive examination is required to acknowledge that in one way or another it is locked into a relativism from which all possible points of entry for externally derived norms have been excluded. It is grounded, as clearly as is the capitalist system it aims to replace, on assumptions of the goodness and tractability and perfectibility of human nature. A similar optimism pervades it. And we have seen the explicit argument from Richard Edwards that "changes in the environment can . . . with changes in the individual . . . usher in a new era."

This, in short, is the point at which the fallacy of Marxism becomes most clearly apparent. It proceeds on the assumption that what is wrong in the state of affairs exists in our environmental context. The things that are wrong are not internal to ourselves. And from this it follows that the way to new realizations and new dimensions of human happiness is to be found simply in new ways of mastering nature and the environment. It lies, it is supposed, simply in new forms of the technical mastery of nature and in whatever societal restructuration can best facilitate those new techniques.

Equally, of course, it cannot be claimed that capitalism in the forms in which that has come down to us from two hundred years of economic and technological advance necessarily satisfies all that could be established as sustainable Christian norms. It is certainly myopic to imagine that laissez-faire capitalism in any form in which it has been observed during this time is necessarily *the* Christian economic system. We have already seen to the contrary that laissez-faire as a system of thought and economic policy is an offspring of the Enlightenment age and the philosophies of humanism and of the optimistic automatic harmony theorizing that came from it. We can see too clearly in history the abuse

Economics, Culture, and Rationality

and oppression, the disruptions and exploitations, that capitalism in its rampant forms has fathered. But that abuses have needed correction, and that abuses will in the nature of things always need correction, is testimony to the very weaknesses of human nature and aspirations which alternative thought systems have neglected. At least, it can be said that historic capitalism, in the sense that it stands for the decentralization of property ownership and the decentralization of power that goes with it, does point in the direction of the biblical norm. For in this it protects the sanctions of individual property, responsibility, and stewardship. It is correspondingly the instances in which this very decentralization has been repudiated, with the consequent concentrations and the exploitation of economic power, that have tarnished and refuted that norm. That serious and excessive fractures in the protection of the biblical norms of equity, justice, and concern for one's neighbor have occurred is only too clear. That a blind faith in economic progress and the benefits of technological advance have gripped men's souls is also beyond argument. And that a faulty equation of "capital" with the right of class domination, and the assumed legitimacy of a tightly structured hierarchical societal arrangement, captured the industrialist mind for the nineteenth and for too far into the twentieth century can also not be denied.

But in all this, the way is pointed not to an even more thorough surrender of the biblical norm of personal responsibility and the usurpation by the state of what the scriptural ethic has established as inviolable individual prerogative, but to a recapture and a widening of that earlier norm itself. This, in turn, leads to a consideration of the status and the economic function of the state and a brief analysis of the manner in which a legitimate economic responsibility for the state emerges.

* * *

The biblico-theological categories already examined suggest that all societal structures, all economic problems and possibilities of institutional arrangements, are what they are because we live in a fallen and sinful society. No point is to be served, nor can scholarship be advanced, by ignoring the point. But it follows that it would be a grave mistake to imagine that economic legislation, at a conceptual or pragmatic level, is or can be legislation for a theocracy, in the sense, for example, in which God's people in the Old Testament economy constituted a theocracy. We do not at this time live in a theocracy in that sense. We live in a fallen society. And we are concerned, therefore, not with the idealized economic arrangements consonant with the organization and administration of a theocracy. We are concerned with the economics of a fallen society. Of course, we have seen that many of the arguments of the Old Testament prophets do provide the behavioral norms against which economic organizations and lawful arrangements should be established. And scriptural sanctions bear heavily on the problems of right and equitable economic procedures.

The realization that society is fallen is relevant also to economic arrangements for providing for those members of society who, through no fault of their own, are disadvantaged by the malfunctioning and discordant inefficiencies in the functioning of the economic system. If modern jargon is to be employed, it is salutary to recognize the legitimacy of certain of the economic functions performed by, or the benefits provided by, what has been called the "welfare state." Certainly it would seem to be consistent with the New Testament injunctions "to care for the widow and fatherless"[15] for the economic system to provide what Catherwood aptly calls a "safety net" for the protection of those who might fall into need.[16] To argue to the contrary is to argue that the classical economic supposition of automatic harmony and maximum economic welfare was readily and uninterruptedly experienced. If, on the other hand, men have a natural propensity to greed, theft, deception, covetousness, and selfish exploitation, then to argue for the automaticity of a natural state of economic harmonies is to be blind beyond the limits of criminality.

Economic organization in a complex society encounters a tension between freedom on the one hand and security on the other. The problems, moreover, are rendered more difficult of

Economics, Culture, and Rationality

solution when it is acknowledged that freedom is in danger of degenerating into anarchy and security is in danger of breeding oppression. Freedom must always be freedom to enjoy economic rights within the sanctions of responsibility, and it is abused when it gives birth to the problem of exploitation or infringement of the comparable rights and freedoms of others. Similarly, security for the proper enjoyment of the rights and benefits of economic freedom is as important and valuable as those rights themselves. But when the price of security, for example security against the ravages inflicted by the malfunctioning of the economic system, involves the trespass of the state or corporate bodies on what should properly be preserved as individual economic prerogatives, then the question has to be asked whether security has not given rise to oppression.

But it should not be necessary any longer to ask the basic question why such a thing as "economic policy" and the participation of the state in the formation of that policy is required. Even though we are deliberately refraining from the construction of any systematic economics or economic policy recommendations, the presence and the inevitability of instabilities in economic society will have become clear. Considerations of the economic implications of the creation mandate, and of the empirical realities of economic structures, make it clear that the God-ordained institution of the state sustains serious and heavy responsibilities for the ordering of affairs in the economic as in other spheres of social life.

Our starting point for the theory of the state is not dependent on a humanistic or immanentistic viewpoint. We do not conclude from observation that the economic system does not function smoothly and efficiently and that therefore an intervention and participation by the state in economic affairs is necessary. From that starting point and in that direction, fathered by any number of pragmatic and humanistic philosophies, lie the pointless debates regarding individualism versus collectivism and capitalism versus socialism that we have referred to already. We start, rather, from the basic correlative data of the sovereignty of God and the creaturehood of man, and on the basis of scriptural data we find there is a certain structure of economic relations and potentialities inherent in the existential arrangement of things that God has ordained in His ordering of human affairs. This order, the same scriptural data disclose, was structured in such a way that it would most effectively conduce to the realization of the objectives of the creation mandate, the development and dedication of all the aspects of created reality to the glory of God.

Against this perspective we saw that although the entrance of sin into the world did not in itself *introduce* the economic dimensions of things, and did not alter the fact that economic relations were inherent in the existential status of created life-structures themselves, it did nevertheless introduce a radically new environment in which the economic aspects of the creation mandate would henceforth be pursued. In their pristine state, economic cooperation between man and man in the development of their respective endowments would have been required and would have redounded to their mutual advantage. In such a state, but only there, the postulates of automatic harmonies would genuinely have determined economic relationships. But we have seen that sin implies the destruction of harmony. This it accomplished in the individual person, and this it does in every aspect of societal relationships.

Sin, in short, implies always and everywhere the inversion of God's ordained order. And for this reason it was necessary that after the entrance of sin into the world there should be ordained by God also, as part of the expression of His common grace, a method of organizing and ordering human affairs in accordance with His precepts of right behavior. It is precisely here that we find the origin of the state and the origin of its delegated possession of powers. The state does not exist by virtue of a contract between men in the manner of Rousseau, or as an agreed means of preserving certain rights of personal property in the manner of Locke. Nor does it exist, as Thomas Hobbes said, as a means of making tolerable the social life of man without which his life is "solitary, poor, nasty, brutish, and short." The state, quite to the contrary, exists because it has been ordained by God to

Economics, Culture, and Rationality

exist,[17] and it exists for the right ordering of human affairs under the penumbra of the precepts God has also clearly set forth.

The establishment of the state as a God-ordained institution for the right ordering of human affairs, rather than as an autonomously contrived institution that emanated from human contract, can be seen to advantage in the judicious observations of Edward Young in relation to the original establishment of the monarchy in the Old Testament nation of Israel. Israel, of course, had been established as a theocratic nation, as the Pentateuchal evidence clearly indicates. But, as Young points out, the book of Judges, for example, "serves to show that the theocratic people need a righteous king. Without a king who reigns under the special authority of God, confusion follows."[18] Young quotes the concluding verse in the book of Judges, "In those days there was no king of Israel: every man did what was right in his own eyes."[19] To focus the real points at issue in the establishment of the human monarchy in Israel, Young continues: "There was a twofold preparation for the kingdom. During the period of the judges confusion prevailed, and thus the Israelites came to see their need of a centralized government. In the second place, the king must be a good king, not a selfish autocrat, but a man who was after God's heart, who in his faithful and just reign would point forward to the Great King to come. Under the reign of Saul, a selfwilled autocrat, the lesson was taught that the king must be one who would reign in righteousness."[20]

We are not here developing a political theory, or examining at length the nature and scope of the political prerogatives and responsibilities of the state. Given the scriptural data that establish the state as a God-ordained institution, it follows that because the "confusion" to which Edward Young referred had a demonstrable *economic dimension,* the proper responsibilities of the state are not exhausted until their *economic* aspects are adequately considered, along with aspects that touch in one way or another the other levels of life in society.

The primary concern of economics as understood from a Christian perspective must necessarily be determined by the demands of the commandment, "Thou shalt love the Lord thy God," within the penumbra of which there comes to expression the second command, "Thou shalt love thy neighbour."[21] Within the orbit of the honor due to God, the scriptural ethic establishes the desiderata of the dignity and honor, as well as the rights and responsibilities, of the individual. On the level of economics, this mandate comes to expression in the respect due to the individual in his capacity as a steward under God, responsible for the administration of his talents and resource endowments in such a way as will most effectively conduce to the development of all things to the glory of God. This means that delegated power and delegated property rights are vested in men, though, as has been seen, all property and power reside in God. And it means that responsibilities therefore rest on men for the utilization of such endowments in a way that contributes to the ongoing fulfillment of society's total economic mandates and responsibilities.

This recognition of the dignity and rights of the individual, and the placing upon him of such economic responsibilities, mean that in the general case it would be a violation of those rights and responsibilities if those definable economic functions were usurped or taken from him. This applies whether that usurpation might be envisaged by another individual who might possess the economic power to enable him to exploit other members of society, or by the state. The scriptural doctrine of the individual person, the rediscovery of which established to a large extent the cultural implication of the Reformation watershed in European history, establishes that *in the general case* his economic functions and responsibilities cannot be usurped. This does not mean that there cannot be any infringement of personal freedoms in the interests of social stability and cohesion. But it does mean, most pointedly in the present context, that very good and necessary reasons must be found to exist before the state can properly assume and perform those economic functions which can be shown to be well within the normal domain of individual responsibility.

The ways in which such a general principle as this comes to expression in individual cases are, of course, very various, and in the fallen society that provides the context for the application of our principles there is room for honest differences among Christian men of goodwill and informed judgment. The following observations can be offered as guidelines for decisions regarding the proper economic role of the state.

The economic functions of the state, we can say, are of three kinds. We shall refer to these as *regulatory, participatory, and redistributive.* The state's regulatory functions permit and require a wide range of activities, which it will again be convenient to divide into two kinds for the purposes of brief description. In the first place, the state is responsible for many kinds of regulations which are aimed principally at the preservation of good and socially beneficial standards of economic behavior and at the inhibition of dangerous or socially harmful practices. The presence of sin in the world ensures plenty of scope for sensible and necessary state regulations in areas directed to this kind of objective. We may refer, for example, to child labor laws, pure food and drug regulations, specifications regarding weights and measures in trade transactions, requirements of industrial firms against air and water pollution, regulations directed against false advertising and consumer fraud, regulations of transactions on the nation's stock exchanges, and many more examples of the same kind in the industrial and financial spheres. All of these, like regulations regarding which side of the road automobile traffic should use, are aimed at the preservation of a cohesive and stable set of social and economic conditions. This kind of regulatory function of the state is, by its nature, generally ad hoc and specific, and it will not be necessary for detail on this point to detain us further.

The second of the regulatory functions of the state refers to a wide range of functions which the government, or government agencies such as the Treasury in the case of fiscal policy and the Federal Reserve Bank in the case of monetary policy, can and should undertake in the interests of preserving the stability of the economic system or its satisfactory rate and direction of growth. Many of the activities adopted in these conditions will involve the redistributive function of the government, meaning both the reallocation of income among members of society and the reallocation of resources among various lines of economic activity. Income reallocation occurs when payments such as welfare benefits, pensions, unemployment compensation, and output subsidies are paid to some individuals out of income taxes levied on others. Resource reallocations occur whenever government expenditures on goods and services change what would otherwise be the structure of the nation's total production. Government expenditures on public works, for example, such as roadways, hospitals, schools, or irrigation schemes, will necessarily absorb resources that in the absence of such expenditures might have been used for other purposes. Similarly, government income redistribution payments will alter what might otherwise have been the structure of the country's consumer goods production.

By the participatory function of the government we refer to those actions by which it participates directly in the economic process by engaging in the production of goods and services. In some cases it may do this by absorbing or taking over what were previously the activities of private individuals or firms, as when the British government "nationalizes" the coal mining industry and all the coal mining firms come under government ownership. In other cases the government may operate a normal business enterprise in direct competition with private enterprise firms providing a comparable service. In Australia, for example, the federal government has established an airline corporation that provides domestic airline services in competition with, and on the same routes flown by, a privately owned airline. Similarly, the federal government in Australia has established a trading bank, quite separate from the central bank, which engages in direct competition with the Australian privately owned banks.

The distinguishing feature of such "participatory" functions of the government is that in discharging them the government engages in activities that, in the normal case, can be regarded as the province of individuals or private enterprise corporations in the economic system. Under some types of political ideology, of course, such, for example, as that espoused by the British Labour (Socialist) party during its terms of office since World

Economics, Culture, and Rationality

War II, a policy of large-scale government ownership of the nation's productive enterprises has been advanced. It is possible to encounter under some forms of socialist dogma a policy of the nationalization of the productive apparatus of the economy for nationalization's sake. But if we have grasped correctly the economic meaning of God's differential endowment of individuals with abilities and resources over which He has made them responsible stewards, then it would appear that the right and prerogative of individual productive activity by the use of those endowed resources cannot be usurped by the state unless there is adequately good reason for the state's doing so. And in that case the state authorities should meet the burden of proof of showing that such a reason exists.

In general, it would seem to be a perfectly safe rule that productive activity should be left as the province of individuals, except in certain instances such as the following. First, and most important, government ownership and operation of productive resources may be advisable in those cases where the provision of the services involved is unarguably necessary from the point of view of society as a whole, but where one or more of three factors prevent an adequate investment of private enterprise capital to conduct the operation successfully: first, when the amount of capital required to establish the venture is larger than a private operator would normally be able to command; second, when the scale of charges that could be set for the provision of the service would not be sufficient to make it possible for private enterprise to realize an adequate rate of return on capital invested; and third, when the services provided confer such diversified benefits on society as a whole that it would be impossible to define a scale of charges commensurate with the benefits being purchased or provided. Perhaps the example of the British coal mines comes under one or the other of these headings, but an examination of the relevant economic data would be necessary to establish the case. Other examples may be government ownership of a railroad system, particularly if—as in Australia where the transcontinental line crosses some 1,500 miles of uncultivated country—it would be impossible for private ownership capital to realize a positive rate of return on such a system.

Other examples of legitimate government ownership may be the provision of hospital and medical services to relatively inaccessible geographical areas, port facilities, postal services, metropolitan transport services, and communications systems. But rather than expand the examples and draw attention to the arguments that would be required to meet the onus of proof of the necessity of government ownership, it is important to consider the legitimacy of the principles we have adduced.

* * *

Our argument to this point has alluded more than once to what we have called the excessive concentration of economic power and the exploitation of that power which can too easily result. It is precisely this, it can now be observed, that lies at the heart of many of the pressures to disequilibrium and disturbance in our contemporary economic position. To take only an example of the questions at issue, but in doing so to bring to prominence the basic root of the inflationary pressures that have dislocated the Western economies in recent times, we can look at the general nature of the wage settlement relations between employers and employees. It might be noted that in departing to this extent from our intention not to engage in a detailed economic policy argument, we are doing so as a means of dissenting from the too frequently heard notion, especially, it seems, from purportedly Christian commentators, that all the ills of our economy are to be traced to excessive government participation in it and to the excessive creation of money that that produces. Of course there are monetary contributions to inflation, with all of the hardship that that causes for those in society who do not possess the economic power to protect themselves against the inflation. And of course there may be instances in which excessive concentration of economic power in the hands of governments may lead to excessive expenditures and inflationary pressures. That need not be argued at this time. The dangers are always there, and no brief need be made now for or against government economic operations as such. Some comments on that subject have been offered in the preceding section.

But there is, on the contrary, no reason to conclude that inflation is solely or even primarily a monetary phenomenon. If it were, then it could be counteracted and controlled by primarily monetary means and policies. But in the present structure of things that is demonstrably not the case. Inflationary disequilibrium in the economy is traceable to the clash of conflicting concentrations of power, to the exploitation of those elements of power, and to the unrealistic aspirations on the part of all classes of income earners in the system. It is this disequilibrium, therefore, with its attendant violation of the economic norms which we have adduced from the scriptural sanctions, that brings the question into relation with the principal concerns of this book.

Here, if nowhere else, a Christian economist should escape from the seductive shackles of the assumption of automatic economic harmonies. For the lack of concern for social stability that drives men to the pursuit of a careless self-interest can only destroy, if it is not arrested, the very fabric by which, in the past, economic, social, and cultural systems have cohered. In the analysis that follows, for the sake of brevity and without overlooking the fact that other forms of cost-push pressures may also occur, the principal disequilibrating force will be seen to be the heavy pressure from trade unions and other suppliers of labor for inordinately large wage increases.

What we have before us is a radically new dimension in the total economic policy problem. And what we need, accordingly, is a policy *tertium quid,* a third dimension of policy, something in addition to monetary and fiscal policy that will enable us to escape from the horns of the dilemma on which we are otherwise likely to be impaled. That policy *tertium quid,* we shall argue, is available in what we shall label, for the sake of abbreviation, as an incomes policy.

In what follows, we are not suggesting a high degree of bureaucratic wage and price control. To do so would not accord with the underlying principle of individual freedom and responsibility we have espoused in the name of a scriptural economic perspective. But we do suggest that the time has come, such are now the accumulated pressures to economic disorder, for new guidelines to be laid down for permissible private economic behavior in certain instances. We call not for the specific control and direction of any person's economic activity. But we do call for new kinds of regulatory frameworks within which individual economic activity can function, to the just and equitable benefit of individuals on the one hand, and the stability and health of the economic society at large on the other.

A great deal depends on our understanding at this point that the price at which a producer will wish to sell an item of output will be equal to his unit cost of producing that output multiplied by a "profit margin" or "mark-up" factor. The economic forces that principally determine the unit cost can be subsumed to a large extent under the heading of the output's unit labor cost. At least, to the extent that we are interested principally in variations in commodity prices, we are interested in the way in which underlying variations in unit labor costs of production will be reflected in changes in unit selling prices. If we can assume, which does in fact appear to be the case in large numbers of actual business operations, that selling prices are set by multiplying unit labor costs by a constant mark-up factor, then a focus on changes in labor costs will actually provide a good approach to the explanation of the price change phenomenon.

The one piece of industrial economics needed at this point is the proposition that the unit costs of production can be decomposed into two principal determinant forces. These are the wage rate paid per unit of labor on the one hand, and the average productivity of labor input on the other. The average productivity of labor refers to the total volume of output produced by a business firm divided by the number of units of labor input, measured, for example, by the number of man-hours or man-years of labor employed during the period over which the production output is being measured. Unit production costs, and therefore unit selling prices, will vary proportionally with in-

Economics, Culture, and Rationality 141

creases in wage rates, assuming, as tends to be the case in actual fact, that the wage-cost mark-up factor is constant. They will vary inversely as does the average productivity of labor. For example, if the average productivity of labor did not change during a given period but wage rates increased by, say, 10 percent, then with a constant mark-up factor, we should expect selling prices also to increase by 10 percent. If, on the other hand, wage rates and the average productivity of labor both increased by the same relative amount, say by 4 percent, then there would be no reason to expect any change in the level of selling prices.

For the economy as a whole, its average price level will tend to remain constant from year to year if the annual rate of increase in wage rates is precisely offset by the annual rate of increase in the average productivity of labor. It can be shown that as a result mainly of technological advances, increased industrial "know-how," better ways of doing things, and increased capital investment per man employed, the average productivity of labor in the mixed economies we are familiar with in Western societies can potentially increase over a span of years at an average rate of between 3 and 5 percent per annum. From this it follows that if the average level of prices in such economies is to remain static the rate of increase in wage rates should also be restrained to between 3 and 5 percent per annum.

But this, unfortunately, is not what has been happening in recent times. The rate of increase in average wage rates, after taking account of fringe benefits included in wage settlements, has been considerably larger than the figure just mentioned. It should follow clearly that the disorder in economic society has now proceeded so far that some policy instrument is needed to restrain such wage demands to a more reasonable relationship with the economy's ability to pay wage increases, or, in other words, with the increase in its average productivity.

It is at this point, therefore, that a national wages policy becomes necessary. Let us look briefly at a set of such voluntary guidelines that were at one stage introduced into the United States during the postwar years. It was proposed that maximum permissible wage increases in any year should be limited to the percentage figure by which the national average productivity had increased during that year. But it was recognized that in some industries productivity would have increased to a greater extent than did the national average. In those industries the maximum permissible rate of wage increases should still be restricted to the rate of increase in national productivity, and the superior productivity performance in those industries should be reflected in a reduction in the selling prices of their output. Similarly, in other industries the increase in productivity would be less than the national average, and with wage rates in those industries also being allowed to rise in line with national average productivity the selling prices in those industries would be allowed to rise.

In some such way as in the foregoing, a well-designed and well-articulated set of wage-price guidelines needs to be established to provide the restraints within which free economic action and bargaining can take place in the future. It is beyond our present scope to discuss in detail the precise rules that might be designed or the exact administrative methods by which they might operate. But it is quite clear that no heavy bureaucratic machinery would be necessary for their implementation, beyond the resources of economic analysis and review available substantially in existing government administrations. Moreover, what is being called for is a set of guidelines within which free economic action can proceed, and not a specific control over specific wages and prices.

But if this *tertium quid* of an incomes policy can be used to get at the precise cause of the disease of inflation that is now sapping the energies of our economic systems, the way is then open for whatever degrees of flexibility become desirable in monetary and fiscal policy from time to time. The latter can then be used to maintain the economy on an even keel in the face of its inherent proclivities to short-term fluctuations and to keep it on a satisfactory longer term growth and expansionary trend.

If the incomes policy guidelines were to remain completely voluntary, the danger would continually exist, of course, that they would be ignored and the system would collapse under the same pressures of inordinate wage and salary demands that have destabilized it in recent years. For this reason, some legal sanctions or enforcement mechanism will no doubt be necessary, in precisely the same way as legal sanctions are necessary to make certain that automobiles do not drive at random on the wrong side of the road. As an example only of enforcement mechanisms that might be considered, and again leaving aside many aspects of the details that would be involved, the following can be suggested.

First, the government might introduce an "excessive wage settlement tax" that could be imposed on those corporations that permitted their average wage bills during any year to increase at a rate greater than the established national norm. The rate of tax, which should be a penalty tax imposed on profits for this purpose, should be, it is suggested, quite high. But the objective would not be that of collecting revenue from such a tax. The hope and objective, rather, would be that such a tax would not actually have to be imposed, in the same way as it is highly preferable that fines for automobile driving offenses should not have to be imposed. The point here is the penalty nature, or the deterrent effects, of such a tax. On the other hand, it may be thought desirable not to impose such a fiscal penalty on business firms that pay excessive increases in wages during a year, but to impose a penalty tax on individual workers who accept excessive wage increases. They might even be taxed to the full extent of the amount by which their wage increases once again exceed nationally established norms.

More important at this point, however, than the operational details is the principle that here we are discussing what, beyond any doubt, has to be isolated as the principal cause of inflationary disequilibrium in our time. And the Christian economist must rigorously face the question whether the stability of the system can be allowed to be destroyed, whether the distributional inequities that inflation engenders can be permitted to continue, and whether the diversion of resources from genuine growth investment that inflation produces can be allowed to destroy our potential economic performance. The Christian economist is at this point confronted with the challenge to consider how well the functions of the economic system, and how efficiently the environmental framework within which it is permitted to function, accord with the economic obligations imposed by the creation mandate. He has a responsibility to recognize the discordances that prevent social arrangements from functioning for the maximum benefit of the members of society and for the development of all things to the glory of God.

* * *

In concluding this chapter we recall the reference in its title to the notion of "rationality." We do so by referring to the work of the distinguished Christian philosopher and historian C. Gregg Singer, whose recent *From Rationalism to Irrationality* provides a valuable survey of aspects of the history of thought or, as he puts it, of "the decline of the western mind from the Renaissance to the present."[22] Although Singer's insights are frequently challenging and highly valuable, it would be difficult to award his economics as high a mark as some other parts of his analysis deserve. He is, however, on meaningful ground when he sums up the relevance of his notion of irrationality in economics in the following way: "As a result of the impact of the Renaissance, the Enlightenment, the French Revolution, and the rise of Marxism and Darwinian thought, modern economic thought has veered from one form of irrationalism to another and from the anarchy inspired by a false view of freedom under law to an equally false remedy in a socialistic collectivism. Both of these patterns of economic thought are inherently anti-intellectual and irrational."[23] It might be useful to note also, particularly in view of our earlier observations on the significance of the economic thought and analysis of John Maynard Keynes, that Singer finds "Keynesian economic theory . . . thoroughly irrational in character."[24] Before we turn in the next chapter to bring this question to clearer resolution, and to do so there in the light of some basic theological issues and questions of Christian belief, it will be useful to note an extended paragraph in which Singer spells out what he has in view in his concept of irrationality. He clearly brings his areas

Economics, Culture, and Rationality 145

of principal concern into contiguity with those explored in this book. Singer writes:

> Irrationality in the sense in which it is used in this study simply means that man remains under his creation mandate to think God's thoughts after Him and to find the meaning of all aspects of created reality, but because of the fall he is unable to fulfill the terms of this mandate. Still conscious that the world is to be known and that he is to understand himself and his role in this world, man constantly endeavors to fulfill this mandate on his own terms, interpreting God and the world according to his own insights, which have been blighted by sin. Unable to find that meaning which God has given to His creation, man has created his own presuppositions, which can only lead him to conclusions which are erroneous and sinful, because they do not honor God as the Creator and Ruler of all life. Man as a covenant-breaker cannot free himself from the requirements of the covenant, and the history of humanism is the continuing account of man's constant endeavors to create purpose and meaning for human existence in terms of his belief that he is the measure of all truth.[25]

We do not need to stay with Singer's more detailed economics, which, unfortunately, although they endeavor strenuously to embrace genuine biblical norms, are derailed at all too many points by his reliance on purportedly Christian economic commentaries that have tended to a false equation of Christianity and laissez-faire capitalism. That important issue was mentioned earlier in this chapter, and we shall return to the point in our concluding arguments below.

It is important, however, to bring into view the implicit conjunction between Christian belief and the economic aspects of our sociocultural position. Let us crystallize the issue in the following way, and in doing so encapsulate a number of the questions raised to this point. First, from the perspectives of Christian belief, and of the revelatory thought forms of the scriptural data, the main movements of economic thought are undoubtedly "irrational" in the sense in which Singer connotes that term. But that does not exhaust the matter. For it is necessary to take account also of the clear and undoubted fact that during the last two hundred years over which the scientific revolution, the technological advance, and the development of economics as a discipline have proceeded, vast strides have been made in the alleviation of human hardship, in the sharing of the fruits of advances in knowledge, and in the taming of the natural and economic world. Inequities have abounded along the way. We have drawn attention to them already. But softening of social consciences has occurred, there has been some undoubted humaneness in the journey, and though, as we have seen, the principal architects of the economics discipline have consciously and articulately turned their backs on Christian belief, social and cultural benefits have unarguably resulted from their work.

Therefore, the need arises to consider the singularly important question, integral to Christian belief, of the way in which, by the administration of His "common grace," God does in fact bring to fulfillment the purposes for the world that He has intended and ordained. Raised to focus, that is, is the question of the genuineness and validity of advances in scientific knowledge, even though the formulators of that knowledge may have proceeded in terms of presuppositions quite antithetical, in the form in which they held them, to the criteria of Christian belief. To the extent that such knowledge discoveries do have genuine significance, as we shall see at more length in the next chapter, it is true that they have that significance by virtue of the fact that the true existential structure of things with which they are dealing is as the Scriptures have revealed it to be. Significance inheres in scientific work, moreover, because it is within the administration of providential ordering that it should come to pass. That, in short, is the basic datum of the Scriptures, so far as they refer not to redemptive history but to the ordering and government of the world. It is also important that the same ordering of scientific knowledge finds application in the area of economics as in every other sphere of human cognitive endeavor. Thus extreme care is required before the work of the economists is dismissed as "irrational" on the one hand, or assumed to partake of rationality on the other. In particular, it is with these more highly

Economics, Culture, and Rationality

informative Christian criteria in view that we accord a higher significance to the work of John Maynard Keynes, for example, than do Singer and a number of other Christian commentators.

Second, the economic norms imported to our discussion by Christian belief must be allowed to determine not only the ends in view. They are rightly concerned with such ends as the development of the natural and economic world in accordance with the initial creation mandate and the sharing of the fruits of that development in accordance with criteria of justice, equity, and neighborly concern. But those norms must determine also the acceptability and rightness of the means adopted to achieve those ends. It is from this point that we can consider in particular the precise forms of industrial and economic structures, the relations between employers and employees in productive enterprises, the claims on production that can be legitimately made by the providers of capital on the one hand, and the services of labor on the other.

Third, the question of rationality in economics, understood now to refer to the propriety and wisdom in any number of such ends and means combinations, must necessarily embrace the implications of the twofold question we have referred to throughout. Positively, it can be easily established that in the very nature of the case the economic system will fluctuate, and production, employment, incomes, economic welfare, and the shares of classes and sections of society in what is produced will not remain stable or invariant. Fortunes vary. And it follows that alert actions in the implementation of appropriate economic policies, in discharge of what we have seen as the economic dimension of the responsibilities of the state, will be necessary. Negatively, the proposition implies that in evaluating the state of affairs from the perspectives of Christian belief we cannot build on the assumption of automatic harmonies in the system. The automatic harmony postulates of the earlier classical economists have been destroyed by relentless pressures of fact and by advances in economic analysis. Such harmony postulates sit oddly with other dimensions of Christian belief, in which the realities of man's fall and his sin are brought to determinative emphasis.

Finally, man's place in the world, in particular in the economic scheme of things, does, as we have seen, contribute in many ways to his cultural realizations, his interest spheres, and his social orbits and preoccupations. In this sense, the economic dimension of reality does have a large part to play in contributing to the philosophic concerns and cultural structures of the age. There is a sense in which the Marxists have alerted us to a profound truth. But it remains true, nevertheless, that such influences are not unidirectional. Happily, thought structures and social, cultural, and spiritual concerns do impinge upon and determine the acceptability of industrial and economic structures. The evangelical revivals of Christian belief in eighteenth-century Britain, for example, bore fruit in the social and cultural advances of the following century, instancing the possibilities that inhere in the reciprocal causation we now have in view. This points, in other words, to the determinative priority of Christian belief or, to put it in another context, to the awareness of the outworking of the purposes of God which are the eloquent first concern of Christian belief. For it is not so much the case, as the Christian sees it, that his belief and his religion are, for him, an admissible part of culture. It is rather the case that culture is a part of religion. For life, in the end, is religious, and existence and behavior move in response to motivations of godliness on the one hand, or of apostasy on the other. We shall return to those deeper possibilities of antithetical self-realizations and to their implications for social and cultural awareness in our concluding observations in the next chapter.

7

The Problem Revisited

The discussion envisaged by the objectives set out at the beginning of this book has been substantially completed in the preceding chapters. Our task, it will be recalled, was first to sketch, in a highly adumbrated form, the principal cultural, intellectual, and economic forces that have together determined the existential structure of the times; second, to examine the manner in which economic thought has intermeshed with other forces to determine our condition; and, third, to consider in the light of these general aspects, the relevance for both our cultural condition and the development of economics of the thought forms of Christian belief. At this stage, a number of the threads of the discussion can be drawn together and some of the principal implications of the argument noted in a concluding summary.

One theme has recurred throughout and brings the differing aspects of concern into coalescence. This is the notion of the place and status, the responsibilities and hopes, and the dignity, sanctity, and worth of the individual. Let us retrace our steps only slightly. In the first place, it was a concern for the individual's loss of his sense of status and place that characterized the pervasive existentialism underlying the "subjectivistic-mystic" attitudes that come to expression in this time. In the context of high technology there is the ever-present danger that men will be reduced to merely animate machinery. A numbness of separation from the consciousness of worth and the subjugation of man the individual to the imagined interests of man in the mass have contributed to determining social habits and cultural orbits. Thus the structural processes of economic production have done much to shape the realization in this time of spiritual potentialities, and the loss of individuality has reduced man from the position of a maker of culture to a position in which a preprepared culture is imposed upon him. The problem of the age, it has been seen in various contexts, is the problem of man, the problem of the individual's search for his true identity and place.

The philosophic bequest that has brought us to this position, and the influence of the forces that have formed our intellectual culture, have locked us substantially into a severely anthropocentric mold of thought, in which man regards himself as "the measure of all things." This has had culture-forming significance by reason that man has sought to find within himself the adequate norms of explanation on both the ethical and the epistemological levels. The upshot of the developments that have ensued, coming to expression in the crassly materialistic-existential nature of the times, has been that norms for the guidance of both behavior and knowledge have been shallowly mundane, and no point of entry for externally established norms has been retained.

These very developments, which have already been explored at some length, point to what we can now recognize as a tension between the notion of the individual on the one hand, and that of the class or the social grouping on the other. The tension is between, in short, the notions of individuality and solidarity. The rightness and priority of the concept of individuality stem from the original constitution of man in the image of his Creator. Although contemporary thought is not hospitable to the notion of creaturehood and the Creator-creature distinction, it is nevertheless this distinction that provides the proper starting point for all valid processes of intellection and explanation. It is from such a starting point that the tension between individuality and solidarity is resolved. For although it is true, as has just been said, that the priority of individuality stems from the meaning of personhood imaged in the creation, it is at the same time true

The Problem Revisited

that man was established in the first place in a viable and existentially meaningful solidarity. This is clarified on another level by the fact that the first man, Adam, was established as the representative of the race. As the apostle puts it in the magnificent fifteenth chapter of the first letter to the Corinthians, we are "all . . . in Adam." As the awareness of both individuality and solidarity come to expression, it is possible to see both the fragmented failures that sin and the fall have introduced to the world and the vision of a renewed solidarity redemptively set forth for men in Christ.

Before looking at some of the implications of this individuality-solidarity tension for issues in economic thought, it is worthy of note that this lies at the heart of a right understanding of the data that determine the Christian perspectives that have been brought to bear at various stages of our argument. For the very nature of the stewardship which, stemming from a distinctively theological grounding, underlies the interpretative framework of economics—stewardship responsibility that coordinates with delegated power and personal property rights as these come from divine endowments—establishes an individual and personal responsibility that, we have suggested, cannot lightly be usurped by the state or statutory bodies or other legal or societal groups. The very concept of stewardship responsibility breathes with the reality and sanctity of the individual. But equally, the theological data we have inspected press upon us the same reality that man exists before God in a union of solidarity. Man in his collectivity is responsible for the ongoing pursuit of the original creation mandate to cultivate the earth and subdue it and develop its potential to the glory of God. The solidarity comes to focus in actual fact by reason of God's differential endowment of men with varying skills, capacities, and resources, together with His similar distribution of endowments among nations and peoples and across different geographical areas. In this way, provision is made for unlocking the potential of nature for human good and for the glory of God in the manner He has ordained. In short, the societal interdependence of men is a part of the initially established existential order. Man cannot escape from society, in the sense that he has been created as a social creature. He is locked to this existential reality as a part of God's own ordering of the ongoing development and cultivation of reality that He thereby instigates and motivates.

It is for this reason that, in the preceding chapter, a corresponding tension between human freedom on the one hand and security on the other was noted. It is the sanctity of individuality and its correlatives of responsibility and stewardship that continually raise the aspirations of men whenever they reach for freedom. This is inherent in the existential arrangements, in the contextual web of which man as creature has been placed. It is only too true that the entrance of sin into the world and into the hearts of men has blocked the way to an unfettered and harmonious realization of the benefits and fruits of that initially endowed freedom. For freedom to be, to own, and to use, has all too frequently been transmuted to an ability and an attempt to subdue, to exploit, and to plunder the collective rights of individuality of others. But it remains instinctive to men by virtue of their created constitution that they should and will be free. Tensions arise, then, not only because freedom to enjoy the fruits of property and possessions may conflict with the corresponding freedoms of others, and because freedom to enjoy the benefits of delegated endowments is as important as those delegated ownership rights themselves. Tension arises also because the demands of security emerge in potential conflict with those very individual rights.

It is a right of individual dignity, for example, that people should be protected, by the capacities inherent in appropriate social groupings, from the ravages of economic distress. These may be caused not solely or primarily by the indolence of people themselves, but by the sheer malfunctioning of the complex economic system and its tendency to generate boom and slump and inflation and recession. We have already given some of the details relevant to these points. But the tension that comes to focus in the present summary is that people may choose, in the interests of providing some anticipated security from the worst of such economic ravages, to surrender aspects of personal freedoms.

The Problem Revisited

This may occur, for example, when people together decide to surrender part of their legitimately earned income to the state or other responsible body, in order that if such economic distress should occur they may nevertheless enjoy at least minimal welfare benefits. Or again, people may surrender their right of freedom to go where they wish in any way at any time they wish and may agree instead to drive their automobiles only on one side of the road in a given direction and only within an agreed upper speed limit. The apparent triviality of the example will suffice to make clear the potential surrender of freedoms in the interest of security, or, to repeat the summary concept, the tension between freedom and security. It remains only to underline the fact that care must always be taken, if the rights of divinely constituted individuality are to be adequately protected, to ensure that in the same way as freedom, on the one hand, is not permitted to give way to anarchy and to the consequent destruction of social and cultural cohesion, so security, on the other hand, should not be allowed to degenerate into oppression or exploitation. It is clear that numerous case studies could be adduced at this point to highlight both the dangers and the possible results that have in fact emerged.

From the tension between individuality and solidarity, and from the correlative tensions and existential realities implicit in it, it follows that care should be taken to preserve the scripturally established norms of responsibility inherent in the differential distribution of resources, endowments, skills, and abilities. It is a myth parented by humanistic philosophic assumptions to conclude that all men are, in every sense, equal, and that therefore equality of shares and distributions in all things should ensue. Such a conception not only flies in the face of what the Scriptures have already established as God's differential, as distinct from equal, endowments. It overlooks the realities of differential gifts of abilities, diligence, conscientiousness of application to responsibilities, and the rewards which, as the Deuteronomic statement of the law prescribes, God also gives in response to the diligence of effort. We cannot therefore argue for equality when the existential order has evidenced a divine provision of inequality. But what we can do, and what the biblical norms are eloquent in prescribing, is to insist that all individuals' endowments of all kinds be employed and administered consistently with norms of justice, equity, and fairness and with a preeminent concern for the dedication of such endowments to the glory of God. Against this, also, they will be administered in a manner consistent with the scriptural norm of love for one's neighbor.

It is true that in an important paragraph in the eighth chapter of his second letter to the Corinthians Paul puts a strong case for equality. But there we have a clear directive to the church as the church, and for the government of its practices of charity under certain well-specified circumstances. The matter at issue does not permit any spillage to prescriptions for society at large. And even within the church as there envisaged, the fact of God's differential endowments of people with different gifts of resources and abilities underlies the possibility that mutual help and sustenance might from time to time become possible and necessary. Moreover, to argue from such a text as this that equality should in some sense be instituted in the world at large is to overlook the other and fundamentally important principle of interpretation we have adduced; namely, that whatever we say about prescriptions for economic society in this time must be said in the light of the fact that our task is that of legislating for a fallen and sinful society. That basic determinative fact needs carefully to be observed. The same point was put negatively at an earlier stage by saying that we do not in this time live in a theocracy, in the sense in which God's people at an earlier time constituted a theocracy. We live now simply in a fallen society. And our economics and our sociocultural prescriptions, therefore, must be those appropriate for that fallen society.

It does follow equally, however, that within the structure of society as we have now considered it at some length, all individuals should enjoy equality of opportunity for the realization of the maximum potential of whatever endowments have been providentially distributed to them. Moreover, all individuals should likewise be permitted to enjoy maximal access to opportunities to enjoy whatever social and cultural benefits follow from decisions to center the provision of those benefits in the hands of social or statutory bodies. Here there comes to particular focus the right of education, the right of freedom in curriculum in education, and the right to be free of discrimination against individuals on the basis of socially determined features or characteristics. Correlatively, equality of rights and opportunities for entry into occupations and sources of economic and cultural activities should be universally available, and here again all forms of discrimination should be strenuously avoided.

In its economic expression, the tension we have highlighted here, the tension between individuality and solidarity, like that between freedom and security, emphasizes the scriptural sanction previously discussed under the heading of the right of personal property. Although no more extended discussion of precisely that point need be undertaken at this stage, it will be profitable to consider in the following section the bearing on this economic tension of what we have now seen as the correlative aspect of solidarity. We shall speak in particular of economic solidarity and of the contribution that emanates from this source to broader social and cultural awareness in the community.

* * *

The concepts of cultural and ecclesiastical solidarity are as important and as operative as that of economic solidarity. We shall speak of the former in a moment. The constitution of man is such that he experiences and enjoys a special gregariousness, and this is as important, in view of God's differential endowments of cultural abilities, as are the enjoyments of the benefits of differentially distributed economic endowments.

Two prominent areas of concern can be noted briefly as instances of the manner in which economic groupings, or the pressures of what we have referred to as human solidarity, have serious importance for economic welfare and generate spillage to social and cultural conditions. We refer first to the way in which economic conditions or the structures of production give rise to interest groupings and to the surfacing of identifiable classes and frequently, therefore, to class antagonisms and conflicts. Historically, the question has come into focus as the "class struggle," to employ the terminology of the Marxian sociology which is again articulate at this time, between the "classes" of labor on the one hand and capital on the other. The second example of solidarity we shall look at briefly is that of the international relations that might well, if consciences are at all sensitive, cause grave concern for the stark inequalities that exist in the distribution of economic benefits, even, in some cases, the basic means of livelihood, between the rich nations and the poor.

On the first of these matters, which involves the ownership and property implications of the structures of production, a small number of biblical perspectives we have already raised need to be kept clearly in mind. They can be observed again without any extended discussion. First, the very fact that economic interdependence is a part of the initially established structure of things, leading, as we have seen, to the derivative nature of human property rights, does itself establish the prerogative and sanctity of private property ownership. Second, the sanctions of individual stewardship that the initial creation mandate involved prohibit the usurpation by social or statutory groupings of the responsibilities thereby imposed on the individual person. This, we have argued, is so in the general case. And any deviation from the norms involved are permissible only on the kinds of grounds discussed in the preceding chapter under the heading of the economic responsibilities of the state. Third, it is clearly a part of the scripturally envisaged structure of social and economic arrangements that there will in fact be masters and there will be servants. Indeed, the Scriptures are replete with mandates as to the manner in which masters, for so long as, and to the extent to which, God has distributed to them the responsibilities of that function, should conduct themselves in relation to servants. And similarly, clear directives are given to servants regarding the duties and obligations imposed upon them in that function. This in no way argues, it has also been seen, for an ossification of societal and economic arrangements or for the impropriety of the migration of persons between one function and another. To argue in that

The Problem Revisited

manner would deny the correlative responsibility for the individual's development of the resources of abilities and skills that have been similarly distributed to him. Moreover, society, as we have seen, provides plenty of scope for its continual reformation, in order that it might be continually conformed more closely to the norms inherent in the scriptural precepts.

Fourth, these very facts have implied that our critique of the arrangements of ownership and economic function cannot begin with the categories implicit in the individualist-collectivist or the capitalist-socialist dichotomies. Deeper levels of motivation and springs of human action have had to be observed, notwithstanding the important and interesting issues that deserve discussion under the headings of the dichotomies we have referred to. Our arguments under all such headings as these coalesce in a sense, or they all emanate from, the initially established obligations of stewardship in which the principle of economic interpretation was found to be grounded. Finally, the scriptural data have established the norms of justice, equity, and fairness, along with a basic concern in the administration of economic affairs for the glory of God on the one hand, and the love of one's neighbor on the other. It is at this point that proprieties in economic action and behavior are finally grounded.

The capital-labor relation, its consonance or otherwise with scriptural sanctions, and the forms in which it comes to expression in modern times are important because of the ways in which structures of production have potential significance for social interests, for cultural habits and orbits, and for the quality of life that is thereby produced. Throughout the development of the industrial revolutions of the nineteenth and twentieth centuries, as only a light reading of the economic history of the period will confirm, there have been all too stark instances of the exploitation by "capital" of others in society over whom it imagined itself to be set in authority. That, clearly, has amounted to the abuse of a God-given responsibility. But it can in no sense be allowed to follow that social arrangements should therefore be so radically restructured as to abolish "capital" as such, and to submerge all ownership claims into a classless collectivity. Those deeper springs and motivations of human action to which we have referred make such an achievement impossible. But it is necessary to note also that social and economic structuration, of one kind or another, and subscribing to one or another set of implicit norms, are inescapably part of the ordained arrangement of things in a fallen society.

When this has been said, it is legitimate to focus discussion on the more detailed question of what precisely might be the arrangements of economic ownership and production consonant with the desiderata we have raised. On this question, a negative proposition might best be stated first. It is in no sense true that "capital," by which we mean here the legitimate ownership of the means of production, necessarily and by any intrinsic authority carries with it a right of an effective "ownership" of the cooperative services of "labor," with which the means of production collaborate in economic activity. We can take the proposition further. It is in no sense true that the ownership of capital, as one of the cooperating agencies of production, necessarily carries with it the right to command or direct or regiment the activity of labor in the production processes, in such a way as would make the latter what was referred to earlier as animate machinery or a depersonalized "factor of production." Rather, it is necessary, if consonance with scriptural desiderata are desired, not only that contracts partaking of the norms of justice, equity, and fairness be established, but that employees be regarded in actual fact as the personal cooperating participants we have just acknowledged them to be. This has implications for the structure of the producing entity in society, or what we can refer to as the corporation or the firm.

In the historical evolution of industrial and financial capitalism, it has been generally assumed that productive activity was to be conducted primarily in the interests of the "owners," meaning the individual or group of individuals who provided the capital for the establishment and conduct of the enterprise. Labor was "recruited" or "employed" by the owners in that sense. The labor force was, it was supposed, purchasable in a "labor market" in the sense that the "services" of labor, even

The Problem Revisited

though not the individuals or the source of labor itself, were purchasable in that way. That being the case, the individuals whose labor services were thus acquired were understood to be available to perform whatever activities or functions their "owners" then commanded, and such directives as were given from that point on pointed to the interests of the providers of capital for the maximization of their profit or gain or achievable economic values. Labor had become fairly completely a commodity, a "factor of production," a definable quantity of potential energy with envisaged degrees of efficiency and capabilities.

Against these conceptions, however, it is legitimate to ask, still consistently with relevant scriptural data, whether the producing enterprise might not be more properly regarded as the cooperative institution it effectively is. It is true that the providers of capital "own" their capital. But it is equally true that the providers of labor services similarly "own" what they have provided. The inescapable economic fact is that here we have coming together different kinds of "providers" of economic services, capital on the one hand and labor on the other, to collaborate in the achievement of certain more or less well-defined ends. There would seem to be every reason, therefore, why improved methods of joint determination of the directions and the hoped-for fruits of productive activities should be achieved.

It is of some importance to notice clearly the form in which this proposition has been stated. It has not been suggested that capital ownership should be abolished, or that "labor" as a class should replace "capitalists" as a class in the ownership and direction of all industrial and economic affairs. Any suggestion to that effect would clearly offend the scriptural prerogative of personal and individual property ownership. We do not need to rehearse the relevant arguments on that point at this stage. There can be no admissible sanction against individual capital ownership as such. It is simply the nature of the property rights it carries with it, and the permissible range of economic functions that is inherent in it, that can be raised as matters of dispute.

This line of analysis, moreover, and the conception of the business enterprise as in law as well as fact a collaborative activity, should be followed in such a way as to preserve the scriptural directives noted earlier in this chapter. This implies that the divinely constituted order of society is such that levels of administration, layers of responsibility, and a subordination of functions are inescapably a part of the structure of things. In the very nature of the case, a hierarchy of responsibility and authority must exist in the interests of order and harmonious functioning in the fallen society for which, as we have seen at some length, all of our economic prescriptions are necessarily constructed. It is impossible to argue for an abolition of authority structures in society in the interests of a classless collectivism. To recall the form in which we adduced the principle from the scriptural data previously, there will necessarily be in society "masters," on the one hand, and "servants," on the other. It is necessary, however, to observe the scriptural data exhibiting the nature of the obligations that properly attach to each.

Given that this is the case, and given that the relevant issues for industrial society can continue to be discussed in relation to the providers of capital and labor services respectively, a further important consideration bearing on possible forms of individual structures has to do with the risks and uncertainties to which the various parties to the industrial cooperation are exposed. At this point, an important asymmetry has to be observed. It can be put most briefly in the following form.

Let it be supposed that a productive venture for the achievement of certain agreed ends has been constructed. Some individuals have provided money capital for the acquisition of the necessary tangible means of production, and other individuals have provided personal and productive skills in the form of labor services. A joint activity and productive collaboration ensues. But let it be supposed also that in the outcome the changing fortunes and vicissitudes of economic developments cause the initially hoped-for gains or profits not to be achieved. In the world as it is, risks are inherent and uncertainties abound. Some person or persons in the productive enterprise must, conceivably, be the residual bearers of those risks. Some persons must conceivably recognize themselves as exposed in a unique sense to the risks of loss inherent in the realities of economic activity. It is true that in the historical development of the capitalist forms of production those residual risks of loss were understood to be borne by the providers of capital. And for that reason profit on capital came to be regarded as in a unique sense a reward for risk bearing. It is not necessarily true that the capitalists were in fact the bearers of all risk in the sense they supposed. But it was nevertheless in this manner that the legitimacy and the vindication of the precise forms of capitalism adopted were envisaged.

It is true, however, that an asymmetry in the nature of risk bearing exists as between the providers of capital and labor services respectively. Let us revert to our supposition that an established cooperative venture does in fact fail to realize the gains or profits initially hoped for. We might suppose for the purposes of example that the products of the venture were unsalable and that bankruptcy ensued and that the real physical means of production that were initially provided by the supplier of capital were accordingly now of no use at all and had therefore lost their economic value. What, in such a case, is now the status of the respective cooperating individuals? The point to be made can be put in rather stark form. The providers of capital have lost forever what it was they had provided and therefore "owned." The providers of labor services, on the other hand, assuming that in accordance with established "capitalist" procedures they had been paid for their services out of the money funds contributed by others, still have completely intact what it was they provided and what therefore they in turn "owned." In the outcome, the providers of capital have lost what was theirs. But the providers of labor services have not lost what was theirs. Not only have they been paid a remuneration for what they provided to the joint enterprise we have just considered, but they still have their skill and productive ability intact and can now reallocate that to some alternative line of productive and economic activity. The providers of capital cannot, however, similarly reallocate what was theirs, because according to the assumptions of the example it has been lost, no economic value any longer attaches to it, and there is accordingly nothing any longer existing to be reallocated and employed somewhere else.

Of course, even in the example cited, the providers of labor might well have suffered from diminution of the marketable value of their productive skills, alternative lines of employment might not be readily available to them, and their precise skills might not be immediately or easily adapted to other kinds of productive activities. Moreover, even if some migration of economic skills did in fact occur, a real cost and economic disadvantage might well be imposed on the suppliers of labor by reason of the social and cultural burdens of relocation and the human disruption it involves.

But the point of the example is apposite, and it should be taken into account in the evaluation of the different possible forms of industrial and capitalist arrangements that might be adopted. In the outcome, there is a genuine residual sense in which, therefore, the providers of money capital are the residual risk bearers, and legitimacy accordingly attaches to the claim or suggestion that they should be rewarded for assuming those risks. In actual fact, it is in this direction that legitimacy is to be found for the payment of a reasonable rate of return on capital. There is every reason why rates of profit on money capital should bear some sensible relation to the nature and the magnitude of the residual risks to which the providers of it are in this way exposed.

But when all this has been said, and when all necessary distinctions and categories of norms have been preserved, it is still true to say that industrial and enterprise structures should be such that the opportunities for the exploitation of one class or grouping of individuals by another are minimized and that such exploitation should not in fact be allowed to occur. The direction in which this desirable objective is most likely to be realized is in regarding the productive enterprise as the cooperative or collaborative undertaking we have exhibited it to be. This, moreover, argues that the managers of enterprises, quite apart from their concern for those whose interests they imagine themselves to be representing immediately, should recognize a variety of other

The Problem Revisited

interests in their activity. They have obligations not only to the providers of capital and labor services as we have looked at that already, but also to the purchasers and consumers of whatever it is the enterprise produces, the public at large, and the suppliers of whatever materials or other inputs the enterprise may be using. It will suffice to refer to the need, again in the interests of consistency with scriptural norms, for honesty in advertising and integrity in dealings on all accounts, and for the recognition and acceptance of responsibility for the preservation of proper ecological standards and the avoidance of needless industrial and environmental pollution. Economic interests, in short, cannot be narrowly defined. To assume that they are, or to imagine, in other words, that the canons of a classical laissez-faire would automatically conduce to a harmonious realization of maximum economic welfare and benefits for society at large is to fly in the face of the large number of considerations to the contrary that have been adduced throughout this work.

This brief analysis of industrial structure points to two possible forms of enterprise organization which, it would appear, might bring industrial and economic relations into closer accordance with many of the norms we have envisaged. First, it is conceivable that at the same time as ownership rights and responsibilities are recognized and preserved, the suppliers of labor might justifiably be represented on the boards of management of industrial firms and corporations and that all parties to the collaborative production process could thereby be represented in all decisions and undertakings affecting their interests. This, in other words, would imply that "ownership" of a corporation in the sense in which that is generally understood, does not necessarily carry with it an exclusive right of "management." Or to put the point slightly differently, it implies that the "ownership" of the money capital contributed to an enterprise does not necessarily carry with it an exclusive right to "management" or, indeed, to "ownership" of all aspects of the enterprise to which, in fact, "capital" is only one of a number of contributing and cooperating elements.

Second, there may well be good reasons why the suppliers of

labor services should be given every opportunity to contribute personal savings and money capital to the enterprise in which their services are employed, so that by this means their range of interest in the economic undertaking is broadened, and a closer identification of the interests of all parties to the venture is thereby achieved. Various forms of participating employee ownership can be proposed and might be inspected in the industrial literature, and details need not detain us at this point. But it is relevant to observe also that even if employees are not in this way participating in the provision of money capital, and even if therefore they do not participate by contractual right in the distribution of profits earned by the enterprise, they might well be given a share in the distribution of whatever profits the activity might earn over and above the rate of return regarded as a fair and reasonable return to the providers of the capital for the risks they have borne. In this case, it would be recognized that the profits actually earned have resulted not simply or solely from the fact that money capital was at work earning them, but that all the cooperating participants had in fact made a real and meaningful contribution to the result.

In the ways we have examined in this section the considerations of individuality on the one hand and solidarity on the other come to meaningful confluence. It is true, on more levels and with more pervasive social and cultural significance than might frequently be supposed, that no man lives unto himself. In the very constitution of affairs, and by virtue of the initially ordained existential structure of things, human interdependence and mutual obligation and help very much determine the proper scope of life and the criteria for its full, God-honoring, and satisfying realization.

* * *

The second example we suggested of human solidarity, with its own precipitate of obligation and canons of right behavior, referred to international relations and the reasonable distribution among nations of the fruits of economic progress and develop-

The Problem Revisited

ment. This question harks back to the manner in which at an earlier stage we indicated the scope of economic problems and analysis as being subsumable under the threefold headings of conservation, development, and equity. Conservation and development had to do, in short, with the proper discharge and fulfillment of the creation mandate, in the context of which man was originally established. The establishment of the obligation to "cultivate the earth and subdue it" has not been abrogated by the entrance of sin into the world. Rather, that obligation weighs more heavily on man by virtue of the way in which, and the reluctance with which, the natural environment now unlocks its secrets to him. Only with a toil of effort are the thorns and briars of reality now subdued to the disclosure of the developmental potential which, in the providence of God, that reality contains. The obligation to develop reality in this manner proceeds in parallel, moreover, with the realization of the differential distribution of resources and abilities which have also been noted as a part of the providential ordering of things. But it follows that the desideratum of equity in the earthly management of this development, and particularly in the distribution of the fruits of it, calls for an even-handedness in the sharing of those benefits on a global scale. For, as we have emphasized already, all property resides in God, and those to whom property has been distributed hold it by delegated right, and they therefore sustain a derivative responsibility for the right administration of it. No property rights in this world can ever be regarded as absolute in a final sense. Whatever we find in our hands does itself, by virtue of its own existence and being, constitute us stewards over it.

The economic solidarity of nations and peoples is such, and it is so clearly relevant to economic policy formation, that no nation can securely live unto itself. The high degree of international interdependence turns on the high degree of differential resource endowments in different geographical areas, and it precipitates a potentially high degree of international and interregional trade. We saw that aspect coming into focus in an earlier chapter in connection with the international relations of the nation of Israel in the earlier Old Testament administration of God's covenant with His people. Specialization of economic endowment and function demands a high level of international trade. To the extent that obstacles to such trading and exchange relations exist, the economic objectives of the conservation and the development of resources and endowments will not be as fully realized as would otherwise be the case. At the same time, the achievable levels of human economic welfare will be lower than would be realizable if a scripturally sanctioned distribution of economic activity and exchange relationships were allowed freely to develop.

These questions become acute at the present time, moreover, because it is difficult for Christian consciences to look with complacency at the searing inequalities in the distribution of economic benefits between the industrialized and the lesser developed countries. One of the urgent necessities in the international arrangement of economic affairs is that ways should be found in which the rich in the rich nations can more equitably bear the burdens of the poor in the poor nations. This is to some extent a problem of international aid, and it would be a pity if the United States, for example, as the richest nation or the one that enjoys by far the highest level of per capita real national income, were to relapse into an isolationism in this respect. But the question is not one solely, or even primarily, of *aid*. It is a question of *trade* and the opening up of new production and exchange possibilities. This turns in part on the export from the rich to the poor countries of economic and industrial technologies and, what is most important, of the capital that is necessary to bring the underdeveloped countries to the stage from which they themselves begin to enjoy an accelerating rate of economic expansion.

This implies that extreme caution should be exercised before a so-called Christian commitment is made to an argument for the cessation of economic growth. For there is enough poverty in the world to warrant the continued development and the proper sharing of the potential for well-being that the world's resources contain. It is true that development needs to proceed in con-

The Problem Revisited

junction with the avoidance of waste and the frivolous use of resources that are now becoming increasingly scarce, and that investment should be made in ongoing searches for alternative technologies and ways of using and conserving resources. But this being given, the international claims of poverty argue loudly for a careful expansion of the production of whatever it is that can be used to alleviate the problems that abound. So stark are the realities in this manner that it would be pointless to digress at length to substantiate them by any statistical presentation. Any person who has traveled in both India and the United States in recent years cannot have failed to observe the tearing distress that abounds in the former country, compared with the high standards of affluence that abound in the latter. This comparison, moreover, does not ignore the relative poverty that can be found within the United States itself. The poverty in the United States is relative only to the extremely high standards of well-being that abound generally in that country. By comparison with India, referring now to the vast masses of people, extremities of distress and destitution simply do not exist in the Western world.

This concern for the international poor takes up again a theme developed at some length in an earlier chapter, in connection with which we exhibited the pervasiveness of the scriptural ethic addressed to the poor in general. This in turn led to the acknowledgment that the nature and functioning of the economic system is such that alternations of prosperity and slump and boom and recession mean that people are thrown from time to time into conditions of disadvantage and economic discomfort. We can have no faith in the classical assumption that the economy is guided by an "invisible hand," the beneficent hand of laissez-faire and unfettered competition, to a condition of optimum welfare and benefit for all. The facts all too clearly belie such a supposition. What has to be observed at this point, but without any extensive examination, is that the same conditions of cyclical growth and instability characterize the international economy also, conditions of recession and inflation are exported from one part of the world to another, and therefore a sensible set of economic policies is needed to assist, from time to time, the maintenance of more stable incomes, employment, and benefit levels.

But within the limits of the analysis we have set out to construct in this book it would be an excessive digression to take the argument further. What is before us now is the need to exhibit more clearly the manner in which the categories of Christian belief do in fact impinge, in a more basic and fundamental or philosophic sense, on the issues of economic health and well-being, and how, as a result, the spillage to social and cultural conditions can also be illumined by biblico-theological categories.

* * *

The argument we have constructed to this point enables the levels of analysis considered—cultural, economic, and theological—to be brought to a final coalescence. Two theological categories, each precipitating a range of issues in corresponding Christian belief, now interpret our economic and cultural condition and throw light on the critical evaluation of it. These have to do, first, with the meaning and interpretative significance of the biblical doctrine of "common grace," and second with the nature of the eschatological or teleological perspective from which our view of the unfolding of human affairs is commanded. In our comments in this section on the first of these issues, it will be necessary to observe its relevance for the actual state of affairs in the economy on the one hand, and for the legitimate nature of a relevant Christian critique on the other. It will be useful to introduce the question with a minimal indication of the scope of the common grace question itself. We shall do this in such a way as to emphasize its relevance to what was set out in an earlier chapter as an evaluation of our intellectual-cultural condition, with particular reference to epistemological potential and procedures.

Questions arose there regarding the nature of the so-called scientific method, its positivistic parentage, and its postulates referring to the laws of probability and chance. Some pregnantly important suggestions of Abraham Kuyper were observed regarding the

The Problem Revisited

"two kinds of science," that conducted from the perspective of the regenerate man on the one hand, and that constructed by the unregenerate man on the other. We recall briefly the critical conclusion of Kuyper's argument and recognize that, as he sees it, the notion of any such thing as a "unity of science, taken in its absolute sense, implies the denial of the fact of palingenesis (regeneration), and therefore from principle leads to the rejection of the Christian religion."[1] It might seem that here we have the end of the argument and that if we want to hold to the priority of the Christian perspectives there is nothing more to be said. Our argument would then be at an end, at a terminus, it might seem, of a rather completely enveloping scientific irrelevance or scientific agnosticism. But, fortunately, the matter does not end quite there at all, and there is no need to fall into this kind of scientific nihilism. Let us consider the matter further.

The Christian apologetic implies that in the matter of salvation and the presentation of the Gospel, a brief view of which engaged us in the first chapter, the Christian and the non-Christian do not share a common ground of reason. It is an unarguable datum of Scripture that "the natural man receiveth not the things of the Spirit of God: for they are foolishness unto him: neither can he know them, because they are spiritually discerned."[2] In the matter of knowledge of things pertaining to spiritual life, there is not in fact any common ground between the Christian and the non-Christian. It is simply not true that there exists a common ground on which they can argue to a mutually satisfactory conclusion the issues of salvation and eternal life. This raises acutely, of course, the cognate question as to what there then exists as a "point of contact" between the Christian Gospel and the world to which the church is commissioned to preach it. It has already been observed that such a genuine point of contact does exist to give legitimacy to the Gospel presentation. But that point of contact cannot, in the nature of the case, be found in any common ground of reason or knowledge capacity. Rather, it inheres precisely in the innate awareness of God, the *sensus deitatis* which all men share in common by virtue of their creaturehood and from which no man can voluntarily escape.

But the Christian apologetic claims also that in the sense in which we spelled it out more fully in the first two chapters, the same lack of a common ground of reason between the Christian and the non-Christian holds in all aspects and expressions of the epistemological process. And it is this that brings us precisely to the issue before us now. The Christian and the non-Christian fail, in a fundamental sense, to share common ground at any and every point of the journey. Cornelius Van Til summarizes this matter in his *Common Grace,* in his conclusion with reference to the believer and the nonbeliever, that "metaphysically both parties have all things in common, while epistemologically they have nothing in common."[3] He enlarges on the meaning of that conclusion by observing that

> when both parties . . . are epistemologically self-conscious and as such engaged in the interpretative enterprise, they cannot be said to have any fact in common. On the other hand, it must be asserted that they have every fact in common. Both deal with the same God and with the same universe created by God. Both are made in the image of God. In short, they have the metaphysical situation in common. . . . [But] Christians and non-Christians have opposing philosophies of fact. They also have opposing philosophies of law. They differ on the nature of diversity; they also differ on the nature of unity. Corresponding to the notion of brute force is the notion of abstract impersonal law, and corresponding to the notion of God-interpreted fact is the notion of God-interpreted law. . . . Corresponding to the idea of brute fact and impersonal law is the idea of the autonomous man. Corresponding to the idea of God-controlled fact and law is the idea of God-controlled man.

It is here, then, that the way is opened to the possibility of genuine meaning in the results of the scientific process, even though it is conducted, as Kuyper puts it, by unregenerate men. The possibility of significance exists because in spite of what might be the apostate stance of men and all that we have acknowledged that stance to imply, the universe is still God's universe, it is still His established relational law that gives it coherence, and it is still His established purpose which the unfolding history of the universe is bringing to completion. It is because this is so, because God continues to preserve and uphold the universe by the operation of what theologically has been referred to as His common grace, that meaning inheres in the world and is genuinely discoverable. It is therefore the biblical doctrine of God's common grace which theologically and epistemologically must come into focus at this point. It is, in short, the operation of common grace that supports both the world and the scientific processes within the world. It is in God's movements and actions in and through the lives of men, even, it has to be seen, of unregenerate men, that there are to be found the very possibility and source of meaning.

The phenomena, of course, that result from the operation of common grace must not, as we have said, be allowed to convey the impression that an epistemologically common ground exists between the Christian and the non-Christian man. It remains true that the non-Christian scientist, for example, still holds to his principle of autonomy, he is still hostile to God, and he still proceeds to interpret his work and the results of his work without reference to God. But the remarkable fact is that he is never able to carry through the implication of that principle consistently and completely. For it is a remarkable fact of God's sovereign preservation of His universe and of His providential accomplishment of His purposes that man is restrained from precisely that, from the consistent and complete realization of his own principles. Van Til again takes up in his *Christian Theory of Knowledge* the important thought forms he raised in this connection in his earlier *Common Grace*. Being restrained by the grace of God from the completed expression of his own principles, man "is enabled to make contributions to the edifice of human knowledge. The forces of creative power implanted in him are to some extent released by God's common grace. He therefore makes positive contributions to science in spite of his principles and because both he and the universe are the exact opposite of what he, by his principles, thinks they are."[4]

The discovery of scientific truth, therefore, is, as far as the principles of a non-Christian orientation are concerned, accidental and casual, but so far as the plan and purpose of God are concerned the same discovery of truth is meaningfully consistent with all that He in His counsel and providence has ordained. Scientific procedures grounded in apostate principles are never able to recognize that it is with God's facts that they are dealing and that it is to His glory that those facts should be interpreted. The Christian and the non-Christian both, we have acknowledged, deal with the same laws of logic. But the cultural and the epistemological dichotomy between them still has to be recognized. It is in the entire area of their interpretation of their work that the fundamental subjective difference between them makes its influence felt. "Weighing and measuring and formal reasoning," Van Til continues in his *Common Grace,* "are but aspects of one unified act of interpretation. It is either the would-be autonomous man, who weighs and measures what he thinks of as brute or bare facts by the help of what he thinks of as abstract impersonal principles, or it is the believer knowing himself to be a creature of God, who weighs and measures what he thinks of as God-created facts by what he thinks of as God-created laws."[5]

The purely epistemological problem and its relevance for our contemporary intellectual culture can be left at this point. For the present, we note only two points of significance that flow from it, both having to do with the economic problem already addressed and the cultural import that that has. In the first place, and most importantly for the objectives of the present work, the issues just raised have significance for the development of economic theory and analysis and for the construction of viewpoints from which to consider the societal problems with which economics deals. Second, they are relevant to the historical development of economic and sociocultural conditions themselves.

On the first of these points, we recall the discussion in earlier chapters of the ways in which economic thought has developed and of its principal substantive as well as methodological concerns. It is not necessary to repeat at length the manner in which Enlightenment thought, aided by later evolutionary hypotheses and a general capitulation to positivism, locked economics to a

The Problem Revisited

large-scale reliance on the assumptions of beneficent individualism, laissez-faire, unfettered self-interest, and the derivative assumptions of automatic harmonies in the system. We have already brought into adequate focus the manner in which those assumptions of automatic harmonies sit uneasily with Christian perspectives, quite apart from the fact that in the historical development of industrial and financial capitalism the realities of the world substantially belied the postulates of the theory itself. And we have seen at sufficient length for the present purposes the manner in which, when economic thought itself became theoretically self-conscious, it set out to construct designedly value-free inquiries, or atheological, amoral systems of thought and analysis. It was of some significance that in doing so some of the principal architects of the discipline consciously articulated their recantation from earlier Christian beliefs, and John Maynard Keynes, for example, and other intellectual historians we have mentioned such as Schumpeter, Hutchison, and Letwin, have adequately sketched the details of the methodologies that resulted.

We have seen, moreover, that in most recent times C. Gregg Singer in his *From Rationalism to Irrationality* has strayed from his primarily philosophic focus to venture the conclusion that, in relation to the areas we are now discussing, "Keynesian economic theory [is] an economic theory thoroughly irrational in character."[6] This he saw as "a conscious departure from all previous traditional economic thought in favor of an economic system based upon government spending and taxation."[7] It is doubly unfortunate that a conclusion such as Singer's, which is not only embarrassingly shallow in its characterization of Keynes's own work and place in the development of economics, but is itself usually put in a pointedly pejorative context, has become generally accepted by purportedly Christian commentators. Though many of these people are in their otherwise valuable work quite outside the arena of professional economics and are bringing the perspectives of other disciplines to bear on their evaluations, such an attitude betrays an unfortunate capitulation to the thought forms and assumptions of automatic harmonies and to the potential beneficence of unfettered capitalism.

The sheer fact that sin is abroad in the world and in the hearts of men, and the fact that industrial and commercial capitalism has developed centers of large-scale concentrations of economic power and an all-too-frequent tendency to exploit that power to the disruption and disorganization of society, make any acceptance of the automatic harmony postulates naive in the extreme. From what we have argued is a more robustly scriptural and Christian perspective, such a commitment becomes, moreover, inconsistent with other and more fundamental desiderata. It raises the danger of bypassing completely the central societal and economic concerns which the scriptural data provide. It is not necessary to reopen from this perspective our earlier discussion of the state of the poor, the Scriptures' deep concern for the poor, the condition of those who are disadvantaged from time to time by the sheer malfunctioning of the complex economic system, and the human misery that results. We do not need to look again at the intellectual history that makes it impossible for us to concur with the conclusion that Calvin, for example, can properly be called the father of laissez-faire capitalism.

But in the light of the "common grace" argument, it is legitimate to ask whether the entire development of economic theory to this point, along with work in other sciences, has contained nothing of importance or significance. Has it not in any sense raised our conceptions to issues and alerted us to categories of genuine interpretative worth? To ask the question is to answer it. It is as true in economics as it is in other parts of our scientific and cultural traditions that distinctions can be observed between the stance, even in some instances the entirely apostate stance, of scientific investigation itself and its precipitate of truth that is, by the supervening reality of "common grace," demonstrably concordant with biblical perspectives. This, it will be clear, is only an application of the biblical common grace argument examined earlier in this book. But a brief observation on some possible applications in economic thought can be made. In doing so, no claim is made for either finality or completeness, and it is acknowledged that extreme care needs always to be exercised in pressing the details that might on a superficial analysis appear to lead from the propositions stated. But that, after all, is pre-

The Problem Revisited

cisely the situation that critical and evaluative commentary on the social and cultural condition is in. The discovery of meaningful propositions in a field of thought in no sense implies capitulation to the inner dynamic or the initial grounding of that system of thought itself.

At earlier points, the classical insistence on the societal beneficence of a rather narrowly defined individual self-interest, and the argument that stemmed from that in its uniquely utilitarian form, have been rejected. The automaticity of the "invisible hand" and the supposedly potential optimality inherent in unfettered competition and rampant capitalism have also been rejected. But that in no sense implies that there is no value or significance in some of the notions of the worth and sanctity of the individual, or in the postulate of the right of private property associated with that classical thought system. That this is so will be adequately clear from the preceding discussion. At the same time, we have argued equally strongly against those forms of collectivist thought which would have the state or statutory bodies usurp the legitimate rights and responsibilities of the individual. The latter turned consistently on the obligations of stewardship inherent in the original constitution of things. But although this is so, we have argued against the forms of anarchy into which individualism can fall too easily on the one hand, and the oppression and exploitation of which corporate bodies can become guilty on the other. We have looked at the important and interesting individualist-collectivist and the capitalist-socialist dichotomies and have endeavored to probe to the deeper springs and motivations of human action that came to focus in an earlier evaluation of our general condition.

But we have not hesitated to observe that legitimate grounds for complaint lie at the root of much of the collectivist thought, even, we have acknowledged, at the grounding of the Marxist arguments for the "class struggle" and the concern for social exploitations that provokes it. We have acknowledged that conditions of economic production and the social structures to which they give rise do influence the range and orbit within which cultural realizations move. And we have registered concern for the danger that men may be reduced by the pressures of an exploitative productive system to the status of virtually animate machinery. In these respects, we have allowed what, from a Christian interpretative perspective, is a completely alien thought system, to provide a valid datum on the conditions that exist and cry out for adjustment. But in doing this, we have dissented firmly from the supposed remedies that the Marxist analysis proposes. It is not necessary to repeat the relevant arguments again to emphasize that the recognition of an empirically valid viewpoint in a system of thought in no sense necessarily commits one to either the basic grounding or the policy recommendations of that system in its entirety.

Similarly, it is apposite to observe that at this time much purportedly Christian commentary has embraced varying caricatures of the work, for example, of John Maynard Keynes, many of them stemming from ill-disguised half-truths promulgated by the economics profession itself. On the contrary, we have found viewpoints of considerable methodological significance in Keynes's work, understanding that a recognition of the value of those insights in no sense commits one to all of the policy proposals which the Keynesians, or even Keynes himself, based upon them. Indeed, it is at this time a matter of serious debate within the economics profession whether the large amount of "Keynesian" work during the last few decades has correctly represented the analysis, preoccupations, and thrust of Keynes's *General Theory* itself. But I have addressed myself to that problem in other places and no extended discussion on the point can be undertaken here. Of more importance for the present is the observation that Keynes did enable us as economists to escape from the strictures of the classical postulates of automatic harmonies, and in doing so turned us back to a clearer recognition of the technical cogency of much of the economic thought that preceded the flowering of the classical system of the nineteenth century. He gave to economics, in a sense, a new vision of a body of thought which had continued an underground existence during that same period of classical dominance. We have already noted the fact that Keynes himself acknowledged the value of the anticipations of some of his analysis made by the eminent theologian-economist Thomas Chalmers.

The Problem Revisited

It is a travesty and a caricature for Christian commentators to dismiss Keynes as arguing only for a collectivization of investment, government participation in the economy, state expenditures, and inflation. It would not be difficult to show from a careful exegesis of Keynes's work that what he set out to do was not to destroy or replace capitalism, but to explain the defects and the deficiencies in the working of it. He set out in many respects to refurbish and reconstruct it in such a way as to preserve it. Keynes set out not to destroy but to save capitalism. And in doing this, the kernel of the contribution of his work, the methodological heart of it to which Christian interpretation can give unquestioned assent, can be simply stated. He demonstrated why it was that if left to itself an unfettered capitalist system will not necessarily provide an uninterruptedly maximum level of employment, welfare, and economic benefits for all. The detailed arguments are complex and subtle. And, as has been acknowledged already, to grasp the worth of this central methodological deposit of Keynes's *General Theory* is not necessarily to commit oneself to all the policy prescriptions that, with the additional aid of various ideological persuasions, might be drawn from it.

That scientific progress has occurred in economics through and beyond the so-called Keynesian period can safely be taken by Christian commentary as a significantly operative outcome of the administration of common grace in the world. The details of the varying perspectives and persuasions that, from that point on, might occupy and provide areas for debate among men of Christian goodwill, cannot detain us at this point. But this issue points to the larger question of the nature of God's administration of His purposes and designs in the world, and to what, to return to the vocabulary introduced earlier in this chapter, might be the eschatological or teleological viewpoint we command in the understanding of it.

* * *

It is at this final point that we confront the high-water mark of the test of scriptural belief. Theologically, the questions of history or purpose or hope take us back to the point at which we began, and they raise the issue of whether we are after all locked in this world into a system of chance and ruled by the laws of probability, or whether there is in all our states of affairs a divine intent. Is our history, after all, what it is because it unfolds under that arc of divine intent that guides the destinies of men and nations to an appointed end? In the last analysis, either men rule as the masters of their own fate but are buffeted by the ultimate laws of chance, or God is the maker and sustainer of men and rules His universe for the ultimately wise purposes that He has ordained.

Within this larger rubric of history and hope, which Christian belief finds securely grounded in a divine ordination, larger questions of technical eschatological alternatives arise than can be, or need to be, treated here. But two points will suffice to bring to final convergence many of the issues of cultural, theological, and economic analysis discussed in this book. First, what, in the broadest scope, is the nature of the outworking in the world of those purposes which overrule our affairs? Second, we revert to the introductory statement that every fact in the universe, and every constellation of facts, is amenable to explanation in its final sense only to the extent that it is Christologically interpreted, and because of the place it occupies in the plan of God. And against this, we ask finally what is the sense in which, and the manner in which, Christ now exercises His rule and dominion over the created reality of men and things.

On the first of these points, we can observe that teleology is bifurcated. By that we mean that the world does not now move to an end that is, as it were, unidirectionally determined. Reality moves through a process of history and time to an end that should be characterized as a double maturation. There lies ahead a maturation of evil and a maturation of good. We have seen earlier in this chapter that throughout the processes of time, God by His "common grace" makes possible the cultural and scientific and economic development that occurs. He preserves His created reality from the immediate and full realization of the fruits and meaning of the sin that entered into it at man's initial fall. He provides societal institutional structures that give us

The Problem Revisited

coherence and the prospect of mutually determined stability in our affairs. Therefore we can say under the Scriptures that negatively God's common grace preserves us in time from the full decay of sin; and positively that grace is responsible for the cultural and scientific and economic progress we realize.

But the time process moves on. At the end, at the final crack of doom, both unregenerate men on the one hand, and God's people redeemed in Christ on the other, will have come to full epistemological self-consciousness. The one will have finally become mature in their apostasy and dereliction from the obligations of the covenant in which God first established them. And the other will have become mature in the righteousness to which they have been introduced in Christ. This is the end of the now bifurcated teleology we have to confront. The Scriptures are replete with the indication, and the teaching of Christ Himself insistently confirms, that in the end there will be wheat and there will be tares. There will be those on the right hand in the day of judgment and there will be those on the left; there will be those with Dives shut out forever in the blackness of darkness and there will be those with Lazarus inheriting the kingdom prepared for them from the foundation of the world.

The exhibition of the scriptural details bearing on these vital questions would require the larger work in theology which, by the design I indicated at the beginning, is quite beyond our present scope and intention. They do, however, raise one important issue that might well be confronted, in view of the misdirection to purportedly Christian commentary that can result from a less than careful understanding of it. This has to do with the imagination that legitimacy attaches to the hope or expectation that the kingdoms of this world will, within the compass of time, become the kingdoms of Christ in the sense that Christian rule and government and authority will have become pervasive and that the earliest of the scripturally articulated laws of God will again have become determinative. The issue is larger than we can digress to cover extensively, or even adequately, at this point. But the line of analysis in view does fail to grasp clearly the bifurcation of the time processes, for the church on the one hand and the world on the other, to which we have already drawn attention. Culturally and economically, the point of view hankers, it would seem, after the simplicities and stabilities of a theocracy in the sense in which we have observed a theocracy previously to have existed in this world. It is reluctant to realize that culturally and economically we have to address ourselves, in the very nature of what is now the constitution of things, to the exigencies of a fallen society. All our social, cultural, and economic prescriptions, explanations, and diagnoses must accordingly be those which are consonant with the fallenness of that society.

The question is a large one, and it is this nexus of ideas that provides the watershed for cultural and economic understanding and perspective. It raises, finally, the cognate question to which we have also referred, namely, that of the manner in which Christ does in fact exercise His rule over men and things while the temporal process through which reality works its way continues. Christ, we acknowledge, is "head over all things to the church."[8] Christ reigns as King in the hearts and in the lives of Christian men. His reign is not admitted in the hearts of non-Christian men, or of those who unregenerately reject His redemption and dominion. And yet it is a remarkable paradox of historical reality that Christ, by His common grace that sustains the world in spite of its sin, and which, as we have seen, orders and brings to maturity the scientific and cultural and economic progress that the creation mandate demanded of men in the first place—Christ by His grace is determining the unfolding maturation of all things subsistent within created reality in accordance with His purpose. It is in *this* sense that Christ now rules as King over all things. And it is in this remarkable and paradoxical sense that the world is in the last analysis the servant of the church, in the sense that all of history is being eventuated in the interest of the church. It is in this final perspective that the Christian now sees his place and his proper stance in the world.

The Christian economist and culturist in particular sees that it is his high privilege to be called to a participation in the unfolding events and processes of the history of the world, in which he can labor with, and by, the grace of God toward a nobler

Notes

2. THE PROBLEM

1. The reference is to Protagoras of early Greek philosophy.
2. For a further discussion of some of these issues, see Douglas Vickers, *Economics and Man: Prelude to a Christian Critique* (Phillipsburg, N.J.: Craig Press, 1976), chapter 2.
3. William Nicholls, *Systematic and Philosophical Theology* (London: Penguin, 1969), p. 41.
4. Adapting a phrase from Genesis 6:4.
5. See Antony Flew and Alasdair Macintyre, eds., *New Essays in Philosophic Theology* (New York: Macmillan, 1966); Stanley N. Gundry and Alan F. Johnson, eds., *Tensions in Contemporary Theology* (Chicago: Moody Press, 1976); John B. Cobb, *Living Options in Protestant Theology* (Philadelphia: Westminster, 1962); David Hugh Freeman, *Recent Studies in Philosophy and Theology* (Phillipsburg, N.J.: Presbyterian and Reformed, 1962), Douglas Vickers, *Man in the Maelstrom of Modern Thought* (Phillipsburg, N.J.: Presbyterian and Reformed, 1975).
6. See G. L. S. Shackle, *Epistemics and Economics* (Cambridge: Cambridge University Press, 1972); the same author's *The Years of High Theory* (Cambridge: Cambridge University Press, 1967); and Douglas Vickers, *Financial Markets in the Capitalist Process* (Philadelphia: University of Pennsylvania Press, 1978).
7. See Gary North, *An Introduction to Christian Economics* (Phillipsburg, N.J.: Craig Press, 1974); Rousas Rushdoony, *The Institutes of Biblical Law* (Phillipsburg, N.J.: Craig Press, 1973); E. L. Hebden Taylor, *Economics, Money and Banking* (Phillipsburg, N.J.: Craig Press, 1978).
8. John Kenneth Galbraith, *The Affluent Society* (Boston: Houghton Mifflin, 1958).
9. See Cornelius Van Til, *A Christian Theory of Knowledge* (Phillipsburg, N.J.: Presbyterian and Reformed, 1969), for an exten-

sive discussion of the epistemological problems referred to here. See also the same author's *The Defense of the Faith* (Phillipsburg, N.J.: Presbyterian and Reformed, 1963).

10. Shakespeare, *Hamlet*, Act 5, scene 2, line 10.
11. Acts 17:6.
12. Ephesians 1:10.
13. D. G. Champernowne, *Uncertainty and Estimation in Economics* (Edinburgh: Oliver and Boyd, 1969).
14. *Ibid*, 1:18.
15. John Milton, *Paradise Lost*, line 1.

3. THE INTELLECTUAL-CULTURAL CONDITION

1. Carl L. Becker, *The Heavenly City of the Eighteenth-Century Philosophers* (New Haven: Yale University Press, 1932), pp. 102-3.
2. H. B. Acton, "Existentialism," *'Encyclopaedia Britannica*, 8:968A, quoted in Colin Brown, *Philosophy and the Christian Faith* (Chicago: Inter-Varsity Press, 1969), p. 182.
3. Brown, *Philosophy and the Christian Faith*, p. 183.
4. Friedrich Schleiermacher, *The Christian Faith* (1830; rpt. Edinburgh: Clark, 1928).
5. John Macquarrie, *Principles of Christian Theology* (New York: Scribners, 1966).
6. *Ibid*, p. ix.
7. See the American edition of this book, *This Freedom—Whence?* (New York: American Tract Society, 1942).
8. Joseph Fletcher, *Situation Ethics, The New Morality* (Philadelphia: Westminster, 1966).
9. Daniel Day Williams, *What Present-Day Theologians Are Thinking* (New York: Harper, 1967), p. 36.
10. See Karl R. Popper, *The Logic of Scientific Discovery* (London: Hutchinson, 1959).
11. See, for example, John Frame, *Westminster Theological Journal*, 36, no. 1 (1973):106, and his review of Paul M. Van Buren, *The Edges of Language* (New York: Macmillan, 1972).
12. See John Frame in *Westminster Theological Journal* 33, no. 1 (1970): 126.
13. Abraham Kuyper, *Principles of Sacred Theology* (Grand Rapids: Eerdmans, 1963), p. 154.
14. Cornelius Van Til, *A Christian Theory of Knowledge* (Phillipsburg, N.J.: Presbyterian and Reformed, 1969), p. 202.
15. Cornelius Van Til, *Common Grace* (Phillipsburg, N.J.: Presbyterian and Reformed, 1954), p. 5.

Notes   185

16. John Calvin, *Institutes of the Christian Religion* (London: Clarke, 1953).

17. Herman Dooyeweerd, *A New Critique of Theoretical Thought* (Phillipsburg, N.J.: Presbyterian and Reformed, 1953-58).

18. *Ibid.*, 1:38.

19. John Maynard Keynes, *General Theory of Employment, Interest, and Money* (London: Macmillan, 1936). See also Ernest Nagel, *The Structure of Science: Problems in the Logic of Scientific Explanation* (New York: Harcourt, 1961), pp. 22-23, on "Probabilistic Explanations," and passim.

20. Alfred Jules Ayer, *Language, Truth, and Logic* (New York: Dover, 1946).

21. Gilbert Ryle, ed., *The Revolution in Philosophy* (London: Macmillan, 1963).

22. J. O. Urmson, *Philosophical Analysis* (Oxford: Clarendon, 1956).

23. H. D. Lewis, ed., *Clarity Is Not Enough: Essays in Criticism of Linguistic Philosophy* (London: Allen and Unwin, 1963).

24. H. D. Lewis, *Philosophy of Religion* (London: English Universities Press, 1965).

25. Ayer, *Language, Truth, and Logic*, p. 37.

4. THE ECONOMISTS' PERSPECTIVE

1. Joseph Schumpeter, *History of Economic Analysis* (New York: Oxford University Press, 1954) p. 9. See also William Letwin, *The Origins of Scientific Economics: English Economic Thought, 1660-1776* (London: Methuen, 1963). See also my *Studies in the Theory of Money, 1690-1776* (Philadelphia: Chilton, 1959) for a fuller development; T. W. Hutchison, *A Review of Economic Doctrines, 1870-1929* (Oxford: Clarendon, 1953); and my essay, "Adam Smith and the Status of the Theory of Money," in Andrew S. Skinner and Thomas Wilson, eds., *Essays on Adam Smith* (Oxford: Clarendon, 1975).

2. From this period the three most notable works, either for their influence on, or relevance for, subsequent economic ideas were Richard Cantillon, *Essai sur la nature du commerce en général*, 1775, trans. Henry Higgs, (London: Royal Economic Society, 1931); David Hume, *Essays, Moral, Political and Literary*, Part 2, Essays 1 through 9, 1752 (Edinburgh, 1817); and Sir James Steuart, *An Enquiry into the Principles of Political Economy*, 2 vols. (London, 1767). E. A. J. Johnson, in his *Predecessors of Adam Smith* (Englewood Cliffs: Prentice-Hall, 1937), p. 9, concludes that "Sir James Steuart's 'En-

quiry . . .' marks the highwater mark of this earnest effort to forge a set of principles out of the fragmentary economic ideas which more than two centuries of turbulent controversy had thrown to the surface."

3. Adam Smith, *Wealth of Nations*, 1776, ed. Edwin Cannan (New York: Modern Library, 1937), p. 14.

4. See Vickers, *Studies in the Theory of Money*, p. 22 and chapter 2, passim.

5. *Ibid.*, chapter 9, passim.

6. See Jacob Viner, "Adam Smith and *Laissez Faire*," in *Adam Smith, 1776-1926* (Chicago: University of Chicago Press, 1928); Lionel Robbins, *The Theory of Economic Policy in English Classical Political Economy* (London: Macmillan, 1952), especially chapters 1-3; Nathan Rosenberg, "Some Institutional Aspects of the *Wealth of Nations*," Journal of Political *Economy* (December 1960); and Douglas Vickers, "Adam Smith and the Status of the Theory of Money." On an important set of questions I have referred to or implied but cannot discuss adequately at this time, questions of the natural order and natural law doctrines, liberalism and the bequest of the eighteenth-century enlightenment, and the Continental contribution to economics in what became known as physiocracy, the works of Overton H. Taylor can be profitably consulted, though they were not written from a Christian perspective. See Taylor's *A History of Economic Thought: Social Ideals and Economic Theories from Quesnay to Keynes* (New York: McGraw-Hill, 1960), *Economics and Liberalism* (Cambridge: Harvard University Press, 1955), and *The Classical Liberalism, Marxism, and the Twentieth Century* (Cambridge: Harvard University Press, 1960).

7. Smith, *Wealth of Nations*, p. 423, italics added.

8. Elie Halévy, *The Growth of Philosophic Radicalism* (Boston: Beacon, 1955), p. 118.

9. T. W. Hutchison, "Bentham as an Economist," *Economic Journal* vol. LXVI (1956), pp. 288-306, also published in J. J. Spengler and W. R. Allen, eds., *Essays in Economic Thought* (Chicago: Rand McNally, 1960), p. 330.

10. Spengler and Allen, *Essays in Economic Thought*, p. 344.

11. John Locke, *Consequences of the Lowering of Interest and Raising the Value of Money*, published with J. R. McCulloch, *Principles of Political Economy* (London: Murray, 1872), p. 226. See also Douglas Vickers, *Studies in the Theory of Money*, p. 6 and chapter 4.

12. See Hume, *Essays, Moral, Political and Literary*, p. 269. The argument as to "innocent luxury" and economic development is found in Essay 2, "Of Refinements in the Arts," *ibid.*, pp. 265-78. See also *ibid.*, pp. 288-89.

13. George Berkeley, *Querist,* ed. J. H. Hollander (Baltimore: Johns Hopkins University) Part 2, Query 229.
14. *Ibid.,* Part 2, Queries 232, 233, 243, italics added.
15. Bernard de Mandeville, *The Fable of the Bees, or Private Vices, Publick Benefits* (Oxford, 1714).
16. Joan Robinson, *Economic Philosophy* (Chicago: Aldine, 1962), p. 15.
17. *Ibid.*
18. Boswell, *The Life of Dr. Johnson* (Allen and Unwin edition), 2:298, quoted in Robinson, *Economic Philosophy,* p. 16.
19. Quoted in Robinson, *Economic Philosophy,* p. 16, italics in original.
20. George Blewitt, *An Inquiry Whether a General Practice of Virtue Tends to the Wealth or Poverty* . . . (London, 1725), p. 50, and contents page.
21. Josiah Tucker, *Reflections on the Expediency of a Law for Naturalization of Foreign Protestants* (London, 1751-52), Part 2, 13.
22. Francis Hutcheson, *Remarks upon the Fable of the Bees* (London, 1750), pp. 63-65.
23. Jeremy Bentham, *Works,* ed. W. Stark (London: Allen & Unwin: Humanities, Vol. I, 1952; Vol. II, 1952; Vol. III, 1954), 2:454.
24. See *ibid.,* vol. 3, *The True Alarm,* for his discussion of the effects of an "increase in national frugality."
25. See David Ricardo's comments on Bentham's *The True Alarm* in Ricardo's *Works,* ed. P. Sraffa (Cambridge: Cambridge University Press, 1951), 3:298, 301, 317-18, 333.
26. Keynes, *General Theory of Employment, Interest, and Money* (London: Macmillan, 1936), p. 25.
27. See *ibid.,* p. 26.
28. See W. A. Visser't Hooft, Foreword to André Biéler, *The Social Humanism of Calvin* (Richmond: John Knox, 1964), p. 7.
29. For a discussion of the importance of Chalmers to the Scottish church and his connection with other theological leaders of his day, see the biographical introduction by Iain Murray to William Cunningham, *Historical Theology* (London: Banner of Truth, 1960).
30. See Schumpeter, *History of Economic Analysis,* p. 740.
31. Keynes, *General Theory,* p. 369, quoting from John A. Hobson and A. F. Mummery, *The Physiology of Industry* (1889), p. 101.
32. John Macleod, *Scottish Theology in Relation to Church History since the Reformation* (1943, rpt. Edinburgh: Banner of Truth, 1974), p. 268.
33. Robinson, *Economic Philosophy,* p. 74.
34. *Ibid.,* p. 71.
35. *Ibid.,* p. 75, parentheses in original.

36. *Ibid.*, pp. 75-76.
37. John Maynard Keynes, *Essays in Persuasion* (London: Macmillan, 1931), p. 312, italics in original.
38. For a fuller analysis see Vickers, *Studies in the Theory of Money*, chapter 12.
39. Steuart, *Principles*, 1:34.
40. *Ibid.*, p. 264.
41. *Ibid.*, p. 266.
42. *Ibid.*, p. 506, italics added.
43. *Ibid.*, pp. 376-7.
44. Edwin R. A. Seligman, *The Economic Interpretation of History*, 2nd ed., (New York: Columbia University Press, 1907), p. 2.
45. Psalm 8:4.
46. D. L. Munby, *The Idea of a Secular Society and Its Significance for Christians* (London: Oxford University Press, 1963), p. 59. Munby's work can usefully be read in conjunction with that of T. S. Eliot, to whose *The Idea of a Christian Society* (New York: Harcourt, Brace, and World, 1940) Munby's work is a rejoinder.
47. The characterization of "immanentistic" has been given to those forms of philosophy that take as their point of principal orientation, or as their determinative and interpretative thought form, some aspect of created reality. Mathematicism, historicism, psychologism, socialism, individualism, materialism, and scientism are forms of immanentistic philosophy. See Herman Dooyeweerd, *A New Critique of Theoretical Thought*, 4 vols. (Phillipsburg, N.J.: Presbyterian and Reformed Publishing Company, 1953-58). The concept of "immanentism" will be used again at later points of my argument.
48. Seligman, *Economic Interpretation*, p. 159.
49. Eliot, *Idea of a Christian Society*, p. vii.
50. *Ibid.*, p. vi, italics added.
51. Kenneth E. Boulding, *Principles of Economic Policy* (Englewood Cliffs, N.J.: Prentice-Hall, 1958), p. vi.
52. *Ibid.*, p. 428.
53. Eliot, *Idea of a Christian Society*, p. 19.
54. *Ibid.*, p. 89.
55. *Ibid.*, pp. 91-92, italics in original.
56. *Ibid.*, p. 59.
57. Munby, *The Idea of a Secular Society*, p. 78.
58. *Ibid.*, p. 79.
59. See James Bonar, *Philosophy and Political Economy* (New York: Swan Sonnenschein, 1893), pp. 182-83.
60. Edwin R. A. Seligman, *Essays in Economics* (New York: Macmillan, 1925), p. 15.
61. Jacob Viner, "Adam Smith and *Laissez-faire*," in *Adam Smith, 1776-1926* (Chicago: University of Chicago Press, 1928), pp. 153-54.

Notes

62. On this entire question, see the valuable work of Nathan Rosenberg, "Some Institutional Aspects of the *Wealth of Nations*," *Journal of Political Economy*, Vol. LXVII, No. 6 (December, 1960), pp. 557-70. See also *Wealth of Nations*, p. 95, where Smith refers to "a country which . . . cannot transact the same quantity of business which it might do with different laws and institutions."
63. Lionel Robbins, *The Theory of Economic Policy in English Classical Political Economy* (London: Macmillan, 1952), pp. 56-57.
64. Smith, *Wealth of Nations*, p. 326, cf. pp. 81, 324. The same notion of an innate impulse or the "desire of bettering our condition so strongly implanted in the human breast" appears also in Thomas Robert Malthus's *Principles of Political Economy* (1836; London: London School of Economics Reprint, 1936), p. 434. In this passage, Malthus indicates his own ambivalence on some important points of economic doctrine: "And in leaving the whole question of savings to the uninfluenced operation of individual interest and individual feelings, we shall best conform to the great principle of political economy laid down by Adam Smith, which teaches us a general maxim, liable to a very few exceptions, that the wealth of nations is best secured by allowing every person as long as he adheres to the rules of justice, to pursue his own interest in his own way." See the discussion on this point in B. A. Corry, *Money, Saving and Investment in English Economics, 1800-1850* (London: Macmillan, 1962), p. 128.
65. Smith, *Wealth of Nations*, p. 751.
66. *Ibid.*, p. 250.
67. *Ibid.*, p. 308.
68. H. F. R. Catherwood, *The Christian in Industrial Society* (London: Tyndale, 1964), p. 56.
69. Jacob Viner, in the *International Encyclopedia of the Social Sciences* (New York: Macmillan, 1968), 14:322ff, italics added.
70. Viner, "Adam Smith and *Laissez-Faire*," p. 121.
71. *Ibid.*, p. 119.
72. On this important discussion, see Viner, in *International Encyclopedia of the Social Sciences*, 14:324. See also the article by James Bonar in Palgrave's *Dictionary of Political Economy* (Fairfield, N.J.: Kelley, 1925), p. 413.
73. William Letwin, *The Origins of Scientific Economics* (London: Methuen, 1963), pp. 147-48.
74. *Ibid.*, p. 148.
75. *Ibid.*
76. *Ibid.*, p. 147.
77. Schumpeter, *History of Economic Analysis*, p. 772.
78. T. W. Hutchison, *A Review of Economic Doctrines, 1870-1929* (Oxford: Clarendon, 1953), p. 50.

79. Robinson, *Economic Philosophy* (Chicago: Aldine, 1962), p. 83.

80. From the large body of literature bearing on the eighteenth-century revival see John Charles Ryle, *The Christian Leaders of the Last Century; or England a Hundred Years Ago* (London: Nelson, 1869); J. Wesley Bready, *This Freedom—Whence?* (originally published under the title *England Before and After Wesley*) (New York: American Tract Society, 1942); and Arnold A. Dallimore, *George Whitefield: The Life and Times of the Great Evangelist of the Eighteenth Century Revival* (London: Banner of Truth, 1970).

81. D. L. Munby, *Christianity and Economic Problems* (London: Macmillan ,1956), p. 92.

82. *Ibid.*

83. *Ibid.*, p. 95.

84. See, for a corrective view, Earle E. Cairns, *Saints and Society: The Social Impact of Eighteenth Century English Revivals and Its Contemporary Relevance* (Chicago: Moody, 1960).

85. See Hutchison, *Review of Economic Doctrines*, p. 51.

86. Quoted in John Maynard Keynes, *Essays and Sketches in Biography* (New York: Meridian, 1956), p. 48.

87. Munby, *The Idea of a Secular Society*, p. 81.

88. See *ibid.*

89. Keynes, *Essays and Sketches in Biography*, pp. 44f.

90. *Ibid.*, p. 242.

91. Robinson, *Economic Philosophy*, p. 146.

92. Munby, *Christianity and Economic Problems*, pp. 4ff.

93. D. L. Munby, *God and the Rich Society: A Study of Christians in a World of Abundance* (London: Oxford University Press, 1961).

94. *Ibid.*, p. 8.

5. THE ROOTS OF ECONOMIC CULTURE

1. Friedrich Engels, *The Origins of the Family, Private Property, and the State* (London: International Pub. Co., 1884), pp. 5-6, quoted in C. Gregg Singer, *From Rationalism to Irrationality: The Decline of the Western Mind from the Renaissance to the Present* (Phillipsburg: Presbyterian and Reformed, 1979), p. 122. For further comment on the related Marxian perspective that has influenced the following analysis, see also Bob Goudzwaard, *Capitalism and Progress* (Toronto: Wedge, 1979).

Notes

2. Psalm 24:1.
3. Haggai 2:8.
4. Psalm 50:10.
5. Deuteronomy 8:7ff.
6. *Ibid.*
7. Deuteronomy 28.
8. Exodus 20:9-11.
9. Genesis 3:18.
10. See the discussion of epistemological attitudes and references there cited in chapter 2.
11. Psalm 73; Proverbs 24:19-20.
12. Luke 16:19f.
13. See Romans 13:1f; I Peter 2:13f.
14. Psalm 104:14.
15. Romans 14:7.
16. Genesis 4:2.
17. Genesis 4:20.
18. *Ibid.*
19. Genesis 11:1-9.
20. Genesis 34:10.
21. Genesis 42:34.
22. Ezekiel 27:3.
23. Matthew 22:21.
24. I Samuel 2:7.
25. Proverbs 22:2.
26. II Chronicles 19:7 and Acts 10:34.
27. Romans 13:7f.
28. Proverbs 10:4.
29. Colossians 3:22.
30. I Timothy 4:14.
31. II Timothy 1:6.
32. I Corinthians 10:31.
33. Colossians 3:23.
34. *Ibid.*
35. John Murray, *Principles of Conduct: Aspects of Biblical Ethics* (Grand Rapids: Eerdmans, 1957), p. 83.
36. II Thessalonians 3:10.
37. I Timothy 5:8.
38. Proverbs 12:11.
39. Proverbs 13:11.
40. Proverbs 19:15.
41. Proverbs 27:23f.
42. Proverbs 11:28.
43. Colossians 4:1.

44. Luke 10:7.
45. Leviticus 19:13. See also Deuteronomy 24:14, 15, and James 5:4.
46. I Timothy 6:10.
47. I Timothy 6:17f.
48. Murray, *Principles of Conduct*, p. 91.
49. *Ibid.*, p. 92.
50. See *ibid.*, pp. 104-5.
51. *Ibid.*, p. 105.
52. Galatians 6:10.
53. I Timothy 6:6f.
54. H. F. R. Catherwood, *The Christian in Industrial Society* (London: Tyndale, 1964), pp. 9, 13.
55. Colossians 3:22.
56. Matthew 26:11.
57. Proverbs 29:2.
58. Proverbs 29:7.
59. Proverbs 29:13-14.
60. Proverbs 22:7.
61. Exodus 22:25.
62. Deuteronomy 23:19-20.
63. G. Ernest Wright, *"Deuteronomy," Interpreter's Bible*, 2:472, quoted in Rousas J. Rushdoony, *The Institutes of Biblical Law* (Phillipsburg, N.J.: Craig Press, 1973), p. 477.
64. Proverbs 19:17.
65. See André Biéler, *The Social Humanism of Calvin* (1961; rpt. Richmond: John Knox Press, 1964), pp. 30ff.
66. *Ibid.*, p. 32.
67. Albert Hyma, *Renaissance to Reformation* (Grand Rapids: Eerdmans, 1951), p. 462.
68. Commentary on Zephania, quoted in *ibid.*, p. 461.
69. Quoted in *ibid.*, p. 462.
70. Amos 8:4-6.
71. Quoted in Hyma, *Renaissance to Reformation*, p. 462.
72. Isaiah 5:8.
73. Biéler, *Social Humanism of Calvin*, p. 31.
74. *Ibid.*, p. 34.
75. *Ibid.*, p. 35.
76. Quoted in Hyma, *Renaissance to Reformation*, p. 453.
77. James 5:4.
78. Quoted in Biéler, *Social Humanism of Calvin*, p. 49.
79. *Ibid.*, p. 62, parentheses in original.

6. ECONOMICS, CULTURE, AND RATIONALITY

1. Joan Robinson, *Economic Philosophy* (Chicago: Aldine, 1962), p. 146.
2. John Murray, *Principles of Conduct: Aspects of Biblical Ethics* (Grand Rapids: Eerdmans, 1957), p. 105.
3. Richard C. Edwards, Michael Reich, and Thomas E. Weisskopf, *The Capitalist System: A Radical Analysis of American Society* (Englewood Cliffs: Prentice-Hall, 1972), pp. 4-5.
4. Shakespeare, *Julius Caesar*, Act I, scene 2, line 139.
5. Psalm 50:10.
6. Psalm 24:1.
7. Deuteronomy 8:18.
8. Leviticus 25:10.
9. Leviticus 25:23.
10. Leviticus 25:16.
11. Acts 7:38.
12. I Peter 2:9.
13. Leviticus 25:14.
14. Exodus 20:15, 17.
15. See H. F. R. Catherwood, *The Christian in Industrial Society* (London: Tyndale, 1964), p. 25.
16. *Ibid.*
17. Romans 13:1.
18. Edward J. Young, *An Introduction to the Old Testament* (Grand Rapids: Eerdmans, 1964), p. 170.
19. Judges 21:25.
20. Young *Introduction to the Old Testament*, p. 179.
21. Matthew 22:37, 39.
22. C. Gregg Singer, *From Rationalism to Irrationality* (Phillipsburg: Presbyterian and Reformed, 1979).
23. *Ibid.*, p. 376.
24. *Ibid.*, p. 379.
25. *Ibid.*, p. 35.

7. THE PROBLEM REVISITED

1. Abraham Kuyper, *Principles of Sacred Theology* (Grand Rapids: Eerdmans, 1963), p. 154.
2. I Corinthians 2:14.
3. Cornelius Van Til, *Common Grace* (Phillipsburg, N.J.: Presbyterian and Reformed, 1954), p. 5.

4. Cornelius Van Til, *A Christian Theory of Knowledge* (Phillipsburg, N.J.: Presbyterian and Reformed, 1969), p. 22.

5. Van Til, *Common Grace*, p. 44.

6. C. Gregg Singer, *From Rationalism to Irrationality* (Phillipsburg, N.J.: Presbyterian and Reformed, 1979), p. 379.

7. *Ibid.*

8. Ephesians 1:22.

Index

Agnosticism, 119, 169
Anarchy, 131
Appalachia, 106
Atheism, 49
Automatic harmonies, 10, 22, 23, 47, 81, 128, 130, 132, 139, 147, 173, 174, 176
Autonomy, 9, 12, 74, 77, 80, 89, 118
Avarice, 112

Babel, Tower of, 94
Behaviorism, 40
Being-in-general, 25
Brute facts, 12, 170

Calvin, John, 34, 43, 60, 108, 111-16, 174
Capital, 23, 103, 129, 137, 156-58, 161
Capital formation, 121
Capital-labor relation, 157
Capitalism, 3-5, 20, 30, 60, 68, 101, 103, 118-19, 127-29, 131, 145, 158, 173-74, 177
Chance, 7, 11, 23, 25
Church, 90, 126, 179-80
Classical economics, 9, 53, 105, 147
Classical orthodoxy, 59
Classless collectivity, 157, 160
Class struggle, 10, 123, 127, 175
Collectivism, 3, 30, 68, 82, 118-19, 124, 127, 131, 144
Common grace, 3, 6, 11, 12, 43, 89, 96, 132, 146, 168, 170-72, 177-79
Compensatory economic policy, 105, 123

Competition, 69, 167
Concentration of power, 82, 95, 121, 138-39, 174
Conservation, 28, 29, 31, 86, 93, 104, 112, 165
Consumption, 59, 104, 110
Contracts, 103, 110, 132
Cost-push, 139
Creation mandate, 88, 122, 132, 144, 147, 151, 156, 165, 181
Creator-creature distinction, 25, 119, 125, 127, 150
Creaturehood, 31, 97, 116, 131, 169
Cultural hegemony, 19, 38
Cultural optimism, 181
Cultural pessimism, 181

Decalogue, 88, 127
Deism, 18, 71, 81
Depression, 53, 121
Development, 31, 93, 111, 165
Dialecticism, 2, 7, 11, 24-25, 33, 40, 46, 85, 118
Differential endowments, 103, 137, 153-55, 165
Discrimination, 3, 155
Disequilibrium, 4, 10, 23, 63, 99, 121, 126, 138-39, 143
Disharmony, 10, 29, 126
Distribution, 10, 30, 110
Division of labor, 90, 94, 108, 110

Economic engineering, 81, 124
Economic interdependence, 156
Economic policies, 17, 114, 122, 131, 167

Economic value, 161-62
Employer-employee relations, 103
Employment, 3, 4, 64, 147, 168, 177
Endowments, 92, 97, 109-10, 151, 154
Energy, 106
Enlightenment, 15, 34, 123, 128, 144, 172
Enterprise organization, 163
Epistemological self-consciousness, 13, 179
Epistemology, 7, 11, 16
Equality, 102, 153-55
Equilibrium, 4, 22, 23, 56, 61, 63
Equity, 3, 5, 10, 31, 93, 101, 103, 118, 126, 129, 147, 154, 158, 165
Eschatological hope, 49, 168, 177
Eschatological perspective, 11, 13
Ethical absolutism, 15
Ethical relativism, 39
Ethics, 16, 80, 119
Evolution, 79, 172
Existentialism, 9, 14, 35, 37, 41, 85, 117, 149
Exploitation, 29, 53, 69, 78, 113, 121, 130, 138-39, 153, 157, 162

Factors of production, 23, 158-59
Fallacy of composition, 58-59
Fallen society, 130, 135, 154
Federal Reserve Bank, 135
Finitude, 32, 116
Fiscal policy, 135, 139, 142
Freedom, 3, 5, 68, 118, 122, 131, 144, 152, 155
Full employment, 60, 105, 121

Gold standard, 80
Government ownership, 138
Growth, 3, 23, 78, 118, 166

Happiness, 71, 120
Harmony, 4, 69, 111, 120, 132
Historicism, 9, 44, 82, 118
Honesty, 98, 163
Hope, 77, 120, 178
Humanism, 15, 17, 19, 30, 34-35, 41, 81, 128, 145

Hypothesis, 44-46
Hypothetico-deductive method, 41, 44

Idealism, 18
Idleness, 99
Immanentism, 9, 43, 81, 85, 118-19
Income distribution, 78
Incomes policy, 105, 139, 142
Individualism, 3, 11, 30, 60, 68, 79, 94, 111, 119, 131, 173
Individuality, 150-51, 153, 155, 164
Industrial structure, 163
Inequality, 10, 103, 153
Inflation, 3, 53, 78, 115, 121, 138-39, 142, 167, 177
International relations, 164-65
International trade, 95, 166
Investment, 10, 58, 96, 101, 104, 110, 121
Invisible hand, 52, 54, 63, 69, 167, 175
Irrationalism, 25, 40, 144
Irrationality, 145
Isolationism, 94, 166

Justice, 3, 72, 101, 103, 129, 147, 154, 158

Kant, I., 14, 34, 36, 40, 74, 75
Keynes, J.M., 45, 52, 55, 59-63, 74-77, 120, 144, 147, 173, 176-77

Labor, 23, 103, 156, 158-59, 161-62
Laissez-faire, 9, 30, 53-54, 60-62, 69, 71, 120-21, 128, 145, 163, 173-74
Laws of chance, 9, 11, 46, 85, 118
Liberalism, 17
Libertarianism, 124
Liberty, 103
Linguistics, 14, 40-41
Loans, 107, 113-14
Logic, 9, 18, 24, 172
Logical analysis, 48
Luxury, 56-57, 62

Mammon, 113, 116

Index

Management, 163
Manorial system, 91
Mark-up factor, 140-41
Marxism, 10, 47, 64, 81, 83-84, 123, 127-28, 144, 148, 156, 175-76
Masters, 100-101, 122, 156, 160
Master-servant relationship, 101
Materialism, 9, 30, 43, 64-65, 82, 118
Mathematicism, 9, 43, 47, 82, 118
Medium of exchange, 93
Metaphysics, 48, 79
Methodology, 46
Mobility, 100, 122
Monetary policy, 135, 139, 142
Money, 64, 78, 93, 102, 107, 113, 138
Money capital, 109, 113-14, 162-64
Monopoly, 53, 69, 113
Moral law, 126
Mysticism, 14, 36, 40

Naive experience, 44
Nationalization, 137
Natural law, 124
Natural sciences, 7, 84
Nihilism, 35, 119, 169
Normative knowledge, 73

Ownership, 5, 123, 124, 156, 158, 163

Parsimony, 58
Perfectibility, 123, 128
Personalism, 43
Pollution, 78, 163
Poor, 96, 102, 107, 110-11, 167
Poor nations, 166
Positivism, 14, 40, 41, 44, 74, 79, 172
Positive knowledge, 73
Possibility, 27, 42
Poverty, 11, 78, 106-7, 110, 115, 166-67
Power, 3-5, 10, 69, 82, 86-87, 89, 118, 121, 123, 125, 129, 151
Probability, 23, 26, 46, 84, 178
Productivity, 140-42

Profit, 140, 159, 162, 164
Property, 3-5, 10, 53, 86-87, 89, 101, 110, 118, 124-25, 129, 151, 155-56, 159, 165, 175
Prosperity, 89, 167
Providence, 88-89, 110, 113, 125, 165, 172
Psychologism, 9, 43, 81-82, 118
Public works, 136
Puritans, 20

Radicalism, 123-24
Rate of return, 162, 164
Rationalism, 17, 25, 74
Rationality, 144, 146-47
Reason, 25, 77, 169
Recession, 167
Redemptive history, 91-92, 146
Reformation, 18, 20, 36, 68, 80, 134
Regeneration, 169
Relativism, 15, 82, 84, 128
Renaissance, 17, 34, 80, 144
Risk, 160-62
Robinson, J., 57, 61-62, 74, 77, 119-20

Safety net, 130
Saving, 58
Say's Law, 59-61
Scientific method, 50
Scientific process, 170
Scientism, 17, 74
Security, 3, 5, 118, 131, 152-53, 155
Self-interest, 51-52, 61, 63, 69, 82, 120, 139, 173, 175
Servants, 101, 122, 156, 160
Sin, 5, 6, 31, 87-89, 97, 99-101, 104, 111, 116, 121, 126, 132, 165, 174, 180
Skill endowments, 90, 92
Smith, A., 51, 57, 59, 67, 69-70, 120
Social engineering, 80
Social gospel, 37
Socialism, 3-4, 30, 43, 68, 119, 123-24, 131
Societal restructuration, 128
Solidarity, 11, 111, 150-51, 153, 155, 164-65

Sovereignty of God, 85, 109, 131
Stability, 3, 23, 118
State, 5, 111, 115, 118, 127, 131-33, 147, 156
    Economic functions of, 53, 135
    Redistributive function of, 135
    Regulatory function of, 135
    Participatory function of, 136
Stewardship, 5, 29-31, 86-87, 96, 104-5, 111, 127, 129, 151-52, 156, 175
Stock exchanges, 78, 135
Subjectivism, 18
Subjectivist-mystic orientation, 36-37, 39, 149

Taxation, 59, 78, 173
Technological advance, 78
Technologism, 9
Teleology, 178
Temporal process, 13
Theocracy, 5, 90, 126, 130, 154, 180
Theology, 1, 2, 7, 17, 72, 117
Time, 23, 179
Trade, 10, 95, 110

Trade unions, 78, 82

Uncertainty, 23
Underdeveloped countries, 166
Unemployment, 53, 55, 98, 106-7
Unit labor cost, 140
Usury, 107-8, 113
Utilitarianism, 73, 81-82
Utility, 29, 47, 120

Value-free enquiry, 9, 10, 29, 79-80, 85, 118-19, 173
Van Til, C., 42-43, 170-72
Verification, 49

Wage-price guidelines, 142
Wages, 87, 139-41
Wage settlement tax, 143
Wealth, 5, 10, 11, 53, 67, 78, 89, 101-3, 110-11
Welfare, 4, 10, 23, 69, 74, 93, 119, 130, 136, 147, 155, 166, 177
Welfare state, 130
Work, 10, 99